FOR EVERY GIRL

Here's to Hope, Healing & Belonging

Solange Tuyishime Keita

❀ LUCKY BOOK PUBLISHING

Elevate International

Paperback ISBN: 978-1-998287-94-9
Hardcover ISBN: 978-1-998287-95-6
E-book ISBN: 978-1-998287-93-2

First edition, July 2025

DEDICATION

This book is dedicated to
Every Girl — To Hope, Healing, and Becoming

From those wrapped in safety to those who have walked through silence, sorrow, and survival.

To the ones growing up in the shadows of war, in the quiet corners of classrooms, or the noise of self-doubt.

May you always hear the song in your spirit, even when the world tries to quiet it.
May you carry the courage to rise, again and again.
May you find beauty in broken places, and strength in the softness of your heart.
May you carry your light fiercely.
And tend to your dreams with tenderness.
Knowing this truth, as I do:
You are enough.
You are powerful.
You are worthy.
Exactly as you are.

I hope your steps lead you toward your becoming—
And your heart carries you even farther.
May you find inner peace, deep joy, and a sense of belonging in every chapter of your journey.

And to the women we are today—
The ones learning to mother the girl we once were,
The ones holding space for our scars, our softness, our story:
This book is for you too.

This is an invitation to go together.
Together in healing.
Together in hope.
Together in courage, resilience, and rising again.

For every girl—past, present, and becoming—
You are never alone on this path.
We rise, together.

TABLE OF CONTENTS

MY DREAM

For Every Girl,

My dream is for every girl—no matter where she is born, what language she speaks, or what barriers surround her—to know she matters.
To know that her voice is power.
That her dreams are valid.
That her future is not a privilege—it is a right.

Today, 130 million girls are denied the basic human right to education.
An estimated 340 million women and girls are projected to live in extreme poverty.
But these numbers are not just statistics.
They are stories.
They are daughters, sisters, future leaders, healers, artists, mothers, change-makers.
And they carry within them a light that the world cannot afford to dim.

My dream is to help ignite that light.
To advocate for their education.
To champion their freedom.
To honour their stories—especially the ones history tries to erase.

My mission is not only to reach the girls still fighting to be seen, but to support the women we are today—those learning to rise after pain, to reclaim our worth, and to lead with love.

Whether I am standing in a refugee camp, a boardroom, a school gymnasium, or on a global stage—my purpose is the same:

To use my voice to open doors.
To build bridges between policy and humanity, between hope and action.
To remind the world that we do not rise alone—we rise together.

I believe in a new kind of legacy:
One rooted in courage, compassion, and radical belonging.
Where self-love becomes our new generational wealth.
Where the next generation inherits not just survival—but possibility.

I cannot do this alone.
And I do not believe I am meant to.

So if you are an educator, a policymaker, a parent, a dreamer, a grassroots leader, or a global partner—this is your invitation.
Let us join hearts and hands.
Let us create a world where every girl is free to learn, to lead, to love, and to become.

Because *for every girl*, this dream is not a wish.
It is a call.
And together—we answer it.

AN INVITATION

Dear women, guardians, champions, and community builders,

In the shadowed corners of our world, where dreams often seem just beyond reach, I am driven by a deep and unrelenting need to uplift, to inspire, and to remind every girl of her power. This book stands as a testament to the boundless potential within each of us—especially the girl who dares to dream, even when the world tells her not to.

I write to the girl who feels her light dimming under the weight of the world. To the one who doubts if she'll ever rise. Today millions of women and girls are denied the basic right and live in extreme poverty. They reflect dreams interrupted. They are stories still being written.

And still—I believe in their power.
I believe in *your* power.
And I hope this book helps you believe in it, too.

My own story is just one thread in the vast and sacred tapestry of girlhood across the globe. Whether spoken in whispers or roars, each voice matters. Girls everywhere—whether in rural classrooms or refugee camps, bustling cities or quiet homes—face complex and unique battles. And every one of them deserves to be seen.

To the grown women still carrying the ache of the girl they once were—this book is for you, too.

For the girl who was silenced, overlooked, or shamed…
The one who was told to shrink when she longed to expand.
The one who still longs to be held, heard, and healed.

May these pages offer her what she once needed.
May you meet her again—with tenderness, courage, and pride.

To amplify this collective journey, I have invited extraordinary women and champions to share their own letters—messages written not from perfection, but from the wisdom of rising again and again. Their words stretch across borders, cultures, and generations to say:

You are seen.
You matter.
You are never alone.

Let us rewrite the narrative, together. Let us raise a generation of girls who know their worth, who lead with courage, and who belong.

This journey is from my heart to yours. A quiet promise made loud. No dream is too distant. No girl too forgotten.

Let us rise, together.
With all my hope and dedication,
Solange
In love and solidarity, always.

Introduction: Why This Book Was Born

I was too young—but old enough to remember—when war broke out in my homeland.
There were no warnings.
Just chaos.
A night sky lit by bullets instead of stars.

I remember running.
I remember not knowing if we would survive the night.
I remember the silence of fear—and the noise of a heart too young to carry so much pain.

That night, something shifted.
And the little girl inside me made a quiet promise:
If I survive this, I will dedicate my life to making this world better—for every girl.

This book is a piece of that promise.

Because while not every girl has lived through war, many have survived battles—of belonging, of beauty, of silence, of self-worth.
Too many have fought these battles alone.

When I arrived in Canada as a young refugee,
everything felt unfamiliar.
The language.
The weather.
The stares.
The fear of being too different to belong.

But in the quiet compassion of a few kind souls—and in a strength I hadn't yet recognized—I found my voice again.
I found purpose.
I found power in my story.

And now, I offer that story to you. Alongside the voices of other extraordinary leaders.

To remind you—You are not alone. You are worthy. You are loved.
This is where we begin.

How to Read This Book

There is no one way to move through *For Every Girl*.

You may read it cover to cover, or skip to the letter that calls your name.

You might underline a sentence that feels like it was written just for you.
You might cry in one chapter, then feel deeply empowered in the next.

And that's exactly how it's meant to be.

This is more than a book.
It is a **companion.**
A **mirror.**
A **gift**—for yourself, or someone you love.

✤ If you are a girl or young woman...

Know this:
You are more than what the world tells you to be.
You do not have to earn your worth or shrink to be loved.
Your story matters.
Your voice is powerful.
You are allowed to take up space.

If and when the world makes you feel small—or life circumstances blur your sense of worth—
let these words wrap around you like a warm blanket.

And always remember:
You are not broken.
You are becoming.

✿ If you are a grown woman...

Read this book as a letter to the girl you once were.
Let it awaken compassion for all the parts of you that still long to be seen.
And when you are ready—pass it forward.

Speak to a girl in your life.
Share your story.
Offer your own letter beside the ones that touched your heart.

Become the mirror she needs to remember her light.

✿ If you are a parent, mentor, educator, or community leader...

Let these letters open conversations.
Use the chapters as guides.
Read them with your daughters, your students, your sisters.

And know this:
The way you show up—with presence, love, and listening—can change a life.

So to you, my friend, to all of us:

Let us rise together.

There is an African proverb I love deeply:
"If you want to go fast, go alone. If you want to go far, go together."

This book is an invitation to go together.

Together in healing.
Together in hope.
Together in courage, resilience, and rising again.

So here is my invitation to you:
Come exactly as you are—with your questions, your pain, your fire, your dreams.

Let this book remind you that there is nothing wrong with you. With us.

Let it remind us that our softness is strength.
That our voice is needed.
That our stories can light the way for someone else.

This is for every girl who's ever doubted herself.
Every girl still healing.
Every girl daring to dream.

This is for us.
And I am so glad you're here.

With all my heart,
Solange

You Have Always Been Whole

You were always whole, even when the world told you otherwise. A gentle return to the child within—an invitation to reconnect with who you are at the core, beyond labels, wounds, and expectations.

A Soulful Return to Wholeness

To my dear loved one,

When I was younger, I often wondered if I truly belonged. In a world that sometimes felt too loud, too sharp, too fractured—a world that could be breathtakingly beautiful but also frighteningly unkind—I struggled to find my place. As someone who deeply loved people, I could not understand how they could also be the source of so much cruelty. I carried a heart overflowing with love, so open that it could not grow the thick skin the world kept insisting I needed.

I cried often, alone and in silence, thinking perhaps I was too sensitive, too tender, too much. But now I know differently. Now I understand that I do not need to change who I am just because the world has sometimes forgotten how to love. The pain I have felt has not made me weaker. It has reminded me that I am still alive, that my heart still cares deeply.

So I begin this chapter by calling you *love*. Not because it sounds poetic, but because it is true. At your core, that is who you are. You are love. Born of love, for love. Meant to shine your light and receive the light of others. So hello, love. I am so grateful you are here.

Together, we are stepping into a journey of hope, healing, and becoming. And we begin here—with a return to what was never truly lost: your wholeness.

I invite you to embrace yourself in a way that feels natural to you. For me, I often place my hand gently on my heart.

Feel the pulse beneath your palm. That rhythm is your original language, the first story your body ever told. Let me start by reminding you, as I often remind myself: You belong.

Long before anyone spoke your name, before the world placed a single label upon you, that steady beat declared a truth that has never changed: You arrived here already whole.

In my lifetime, I have held newborns—my own children and others around the world in remote villages and makeshift clinics. I have watched their tiny chests rise and fall with the same sacred rhythm. And every time I have held a child, I have whispered the same silent truth: You don't need to earn your worth.

No certificate of belonging is required. No achievement necessary to prove your right to be here. Every child begins as an unrepeatable miracle.

Somewhere along the way, though, the world starts to whisper lies. Maybe it was a parent too overwhelmed to notice your brilliance. Or a teacher who shamed your curiosity. Maybe it was illness, war, poverty, loss—experiences that cracked your sense of safety. The world, in all its chaos, begins to fracture the story you once knew in your bones. And slowly, almost without realizing, we begin to question ourselves: *Am I lovable? Am I safe? Do I matter?*

If trauma is disconnection, then healing is reconnection. And that is the invitation of this part of your journey: to return. To remember. To reconnect with the part of you that never stopped being whole.

The First Mirror

As children, our first mirror is supposed to reflect back one simple truth:
"I exist. I am safe. I am loved."

But maybe your mirror cracked early. Perhaps a parent was overwhelmed, or a teacher shamed your questions, or violence thundered through your neighborhood before you had words to explain it. Your tiny body—brilliant and resourceful—responded the only way it knew: it adapted.

You might have become the Quiet One, tiptoeing through life so no one would notice the chaos inside your home. Or the Funny One, turning pain into punchlines so the room could exhale. Or the Perfect One, believing that flawless grades or spotless dishes could guarantee love.

Those responses weren't failures; they were genius.
They kept you safe.
Each adaptation was brilliant. Each was brave.

And yet, behind every adaptation lived a silent agreement: *"I will trade pieces of my real self for the illusion of safety. I will dim to belong."* And over time, you may have forgotten where you ended and the coping began.

But here's the truth: Your nervous system is not your enemy. It is your loyal bodyguard, your lifelong companion. The anxiety you feel without warning? The fatigue that sleep doesn't touch? The ache in your chest where tears once lived?

None of these mean you are broken. They mean your body remembers. They mean your spirit protected you the best way it knew how. They mean you survived. And the good news is anything learned can be unlearned. Wholeness is not lost; it is simply waiting underneath the layers we used to survive.

Part I of our journey invites you to gather scattered pieces of your story and begin stitching them together with compassion. You will sense, perhaps for the first time in a long while, that your body can be a home—not just a shelter from storms but a place where sunlight streams in.

May you feel the love of a promise kept:
you have always been whole.

Let's begin.

To the Girl I Was, and the Girl You Are

There is a little girl I still carry in my heart.

She was eleven when war found her.
She ran with her family—empty-handed, terrified—never knowing if morning would come.
She didn't speak for days after watching the world collapse.
She held her dreams like tiny pebbles in her pocket—quietly, tightly—because even dreams can be stolen when the world forgets you exist.

That girl was me.
And maybe, in some way… that girl is also you.

Maybe you're the girl who had to grow up too fast.
Or the girl who always feels like she's too much—or not enough.
Maybe you've been told to stay small, stay quiet, be perfect, or disappear.
Maybe you're the girl looking in the mirror wondering:
Where do I belong? Who am I allowed to be?

Or maybe you're just waiting for someone to notice:
That you're trying.
That you're still here.
That you still care.

This book is for you.

It's a letter of love, stitched together with stories and lessons from women who have walked through fire—and somehow kept the light inside them burning.
It's a collection of wisdom from leaders who dared to be kind in a world that demanded toughness.
It's a hand reaching back to say:
Come with me. There's room for you too.

In these pages, you'll hear from women who've become presidents, mothers, doctors, artists, teachers, and changemakers.
They write not only to their younger selves—but to you.

To the girl you are.
To the girl you're becoming.

Some letters will feel like a warm hug.
Some will stir tears you didn't know were waiting.
Some will sound like a friend who finally gets it.

And after each letter, I will meet you again—with stories, life lessons, and gentle tools to walk beside you.
Because even on the days you feel small,
I want you to remember:

Your voice matters—even if it trembles.
Your story is worthy—even if it's still unfolding.
Your dreams are sacred—even if no one claps for them yet.
You, too, may be carrying your dreams like pebbles.
May this book remind you it's safe to let them shine.

This book was born from the girl I was, and the woman I became—
because I promised her long ago:
If we make it through, we will make it matter.

So now, I hand this book to you.

To the girl who dares to dream.
To the girl who's been through too much.
To the girl searching for hope, for healing, for home—

We are here.
We are with you.
And we are just getting started.

PART I

Embody: Remember Your Wholeness

You were always whole, even when the world told you otherwise.

A gentle return to the child within—an invitation to reconnect with who we are at the core, beyond labels, wounds, and expectations.

CHAPTER 1

To the Girl Who Feels Like a Stranger —

You are not lost—you are learning how to build a home, because you are uniquely needed in this world.

I see the way you scan a room, wondering whether there is space for you. Questions bloom quietly in your chest—Do I belong? Am I too different? Too quiet? Too much? You notice what others rush past; you feel what they ignore. That is not a flaw. That is your gift.

Belonging is not about being chosen by everyone. It is about choosing yourself, even when the world does not understand your language. You were never meant to fit every corner—you were meant to shape one where kindness lives and people can breathe again.

Some days it feels as if you woke inside someone else's dream, wandering through streets that do not speak your name. That ache—the pull toward something softer, truer, safer—is not proof that you are lost. It is proof that you remember what love feels like. You refuse to forget.

Yes, feeling at home may take time. Perhaps that is because you are the one meant to create it. You are becoming the place others will one day run to for shelter. The quiet you hold is wisdom; the tears you hide are prayers in motion. You are not too sensitive—you are paying attention.

So please, do not trade your quiet for their noise. Do not shrink the parts of you that still sing in the voice of your ancestors, or unlearn your dreams to cushion someone else's comfort. This world has forgotten what softness looks like, but you are not here to be hardened; you are here to build something softer.

You are not too different. You are the difference—a living bridge between what was and what could be. Even when your accent feels heavy, when no one pronounces your name the way it was meant to be sung, remember this: you are not becoming someone new; you are returning to who you have always been. And who you are is already enough.

One day, someone will step into a room and find home in your presence. Until then, build that home within yourself—with softness, with truth, with the grace to be exactly who you are.

You are not lost, my love.
You are on your way home.

With all my heart,
The one who sees you and loves you immensely

Life Lesson:
Create Belonging When You Feel Like a Stranger

You are not lost. You are learning how to build a home—because you carry the kind of light this world does not yet know how to hold.

Let me begin with a story. Not because it is rare, but because it is far too common.

The first time I left my birth home, I was still a child. Like many children, I believed we would return soon. I thought the life we knew would wait for us. But the journey did not lead back to familiarity. Instead, I found myself sleeping in a tent, surrounded by other refugees, the sound of grief hanging in the night like a second sky. I went from having everything to suddenly having nothing.

In the days, months, and years that followed, I often wondered if I would ever feel at home again—not just in a country or a classroom, but in my own skin, in my own name, in my own story.

When I arrived in a new country as a child, the world felt upside down. The snow looked like powdered sugar, but it bit my skin as if it resented me for being there. My name, once music in my mother's mouth, became a stumbling block in classrooms and roll calls. People looked at me with polite curiosity, as if I were a walking question. I smiled a lot. Not because I felt at ease, but because I was trying to translate myself through kindness.

Back then, I did not have the words for what I felt. I only knew the ache. I sat alone at lunch, pretending not to notice. I lowered my voice to match the accents around me. I laughed at jokes I did not understand. I tried to be easy to like—easier to explain.

But beneath the surface, I longed for a softness I quietly hoped to find again. I missed the cadence of my grandmother's voice.

I missed the warmth of my name in my family's prayers. I missed the girl I had been before I realized how different I was.

This is a story many of us carry. Whether we have crossed oceans or simply walked into rooms where no one quite sees us, we know what it feels like to scan the world for signs of safety. We know what it feels like to wonder: *Am I too much? Am I not enough?*

But here is what I have learned: feeling like a stranger does not mean you do not belong. It simply means the world has not yet caught up to the kind of beauty and value you carry. You are not here to be reshaped to fit every mold. You are here to create a space that reflects your heart.

Belonging Is Not About Fitting In

We are often taught that belonging comes from being liked, accepted, or applauded. But fitting in is not belonging—it is performance. It is shrinking, adjusting, and hoping someone else will finally say, *Yes, you may stay.*

True belonging begins within. It begins when you give yourself permission to take up space—as you are, not as the world prefers you to be.

That is not easy, especially when your difference has been used against you. Perhaps your accent made someone laugh. Perhaps your clothes did not follow the trend. Perhaps you dream differently, believe differently, or love differently. And so, you begin to think: *If I could just soften the edges, maybe they'd let me in.*

But love, those edges are what make you Whole.

You were not made to disappear inside someone else's version of home.

The truth is, you are not a guest here. You are a builder. A creator. A seed-planter. One day, others will thank you for showing them another way to live—with more kindness, with more truth.

The Ache of Not Belonging Is Not Your Fault

There is a specific kind of pain that comes from being misunderstood. It can make you second-guess your voice, your story, and your worth. It can make you wonder if you should speak at all.

When the world mirrors back confusion instead of acceptance, it is easy to believe that you are the one who needs to change. But you do not. What you need is a mirror that reflects back love. And when that mirror does not exist in the room you are in, you must begin building it within yourself.

That is the quiet, courageous work of creating belonging.

What Building a Home Feels Like

Building a home within yourself does not always feel poetic or graceful. Some days, it looks like putting on your favorite dress—the one that makes you feel alive. Some days, it means writing your full name across a blank page and reading it aloud until it feels like truth again.

One evening, I wrote my name—middle syllables and all—in a fresh journal. Beneath it, I wrote: *You do not owe anyone an easier version of yourself.* I read it again and again until the words felt like they belonged to me.

Creating home is about finding people who truly see you—and also becoming someone who sees yourself. It is dressing in a way that reflects your spirit, even if it raises eyebrows. It is cooking food from your culture or embracing new ones without apology. It is letting your silence speak volumes. It is allowing your softness to remain intact.

It is reclaiming your story.

You are not broken for feeling out of place. You are waking up to the truth: belonging is not something given. It is something created.

Reflections That Lead You Home

Instead of rushing to find answers, pause and listen inward. These are not questions you need to solve. They are doors you gently open.

- When was the first time you felt like a stranger? And who were you before that moment asked you to shrink?

- What places—real or remembered—help you breathe a little easier?

- Who helps you feel more like yourself, without needing to explain?

- What rituals—no matter how small—help you feel grounded and known? A cup of tea? A song in your language? Your full name, spoken aloud in a safe space?

- If you could build a home that held all of you—your memories, your mistakes, your dreams—what would it feel like? Who would be welcome there?

Let your answers be a doorway back to yourself.

A Letter to My Younger Self

Sweet girl,

You did not need to laugh at jokes that hurt. You did not need to nod when your name was mispronounced. You did not need to stay quiet to make others comfortable.

I am sorry no one told you sooner. You belong—not because you adjusted, but because you exist. Not because someone said you are worthy, but because your worth was never in question.

I love the girl you were—the one who twisted and stretched herself just to be accepted. You believed that if you could just fit, someone might finally say you mattered.

You always did. You still do.

You are not strange. You are sacred. You do not need to earn your place. You already are the place. Keep coming home.

The Quiet Truth That Travels

Here is the truth I carry now: I am not too much. I am not too sensitive. I am not too different.

I am simply aware—in a world that has forgotten
how to pay attention.
I am tender—in a world that confuses loudness with leadership.
I am honest—in a world that often rewards performance.

The world may not always make room. But it cannot stop you from setting your own table—full of story, full of flavor, full of presence.

Belonging that requires performance is always conditional. But the kind you build from truth? That kind lasts.
You do not need to change. You need only to remember what is already true inside you.

Because remembering is how we find our way back home.

Keep Going, Love

If these words feel distant, let them sit beside you until they feel familiar. Belief does not have to be loud to be real. Like breath, it only needs to return.

So start softly. Begin where you are.

Think of the spaces—real or imagined—where your soul exhales. Think of the people who do not flinch at your fullness. Think of the rituals that remind you that you are already whole.

You do not have to pretend that certain jokes do not hurt. You do not have to erase your name to be respected. You do not have to make yourself small to keep others comfortable.

You were always worthy. Not because someone said so.
But because you are here.
Breathing. Becoming.

You are not strange. You are sacred.
You are not too much. You are enough.
You are not broken. You are remembering.

And that remembering, love—that is your homecoming.

You carry the memory of a better world.
You carry the whisper of healing.
You carry the light of what is possible.

So plant. Water. Stay.

The home you are building is already taking root.

You are not lost, my love.
You are on your way home.

Tools for the Journey:
Come Home to Belonging

If these words feel distant, let them sit beside you until they feel familiar. Belief does not have to be loud to be real. Like breath, it only needs to return.

So start softly. Begin where you are.

Think of the spaces—real or imagined—where your soul exhales. Think of the people who do not flinch at your fullness. Think of the rituals that remind you that you are already whole.

You do not have to pretend that certain jokes do not hurt. You do not have to erase your name to be respected. You do not have to make yourself small to keep others comfortable.

You were always worthy. Not because someone said so.
But because you are here.
Breathing. Becoming.

You are not strange. You are sacred.
You are not too much. You are enough.
You are not broken. You are remembering.

And that remembering, love—that is your homecoming.

You carry the memory of a better world.
You carry the whisper of healing.
You carry the light of what is possible.

So plant. Water. Stay.

The home you are building is already taking root.

You are not lost, my love.
You are on your way home.

CHAPTER 2

To the Girl Who Wonders If She Matters —

Your presence is not just wanted. It is needed.

You have been quiet—not because you have nothing to say, but because you have been wondering if anyone would notice if you stopped saying it.
You walk through the world like a question mark, unsure if your voice adds anything, unsure if your presence makes a difference.

I want you to know that you are seen—I see you.

If no one has said it in a while—or maybe ever—I hope you let these words settle gently inside you: **You are seen.**

Not just by me, but by the quiet rhythm of life itself— the one that has carried you from moment to moment, even when the world seemed to look the other way.

Sometimes, we move through spaces where our worth isn't mirrored back to us, and that absence can feel louder than anything else. But even in the quiet, even when you are unsure, you are not invisible.

In the stillness between your thoughts, in the breath that keeps rising, in the simple, courageous act of *still being here*—**you are already enough.** You matter, not because of what you do, or how you shine on someone else's scale, but because of who you are when no one is watching.

That presence—your presence—is not just valuable. It is necessary. It is a blessing in motion.

You are not invisible, even if the world sometimes acts like you are. You are not a shadow. You are not a burden. You are a light—soft, steady, and irreplaceable.

I know what it feels like to sit in a crowded room and believe that your absence wouldn't change a thing. I have been the girl who tried to take up less space, thinking that would make people stay.`

The world does not need a quieter version of you. It needs **you**—the real you. The one who feels deeply, loves quietly, and notices what others overlook. That is not weakness, that is your power.

There is something about you that can never be replicated. The way you listen. The way you hold space. The way your eyes soften when someone is hurting. That kind of presence changes people, even if they never find the words to thank you.

So please—don't disappear. Do not fold yourself up just to fit into someone else's comfort. Do not doubt your worth just because someone else couldn't see it.

The truth will always be that: Your presence is a thread in someone else's healing. Your voice may be the echo someone else needs to feel less alone. And while you may never know the full impact of your kindness, your gentleness, your being; it will always matters. **You will always matter.**

Even when it feels like no one is watching, your existence is a quiet revolution. Your breath is a poem. Your presence is a seed.

So stay.

Stay in the room. Stay in your body. Stay in the story. The world is already better because you are in it.

With all my heart,
The one who will never stop believing in you

Life Lesson:
You Matter More Than You Know

Sometimes, the deepest kind of loneliness does not come when we are physically alone.
It comes when we are surrounded by people—and still feel unseen.

After surviving conflict and genocide, I lived in survival mode for years. From childhood into adulthood, I kept moving. I kept achieving. I kept proving—to others, and perhaps to myself—that I was still here. Still worthy. I stayed busy because, somewhere deep and hidden, I believed that my productivity justified my existence.

But beneath all that motion was a quiet fear: if I ever slowed down, the silence might reveal a grief too vast to hold. The pain I had buried might rise to the surface—and I wasn't sure I was ready to meet it.

So I filled every hour. Every calendar square. Every inch inside me. With doing. With striving. With staying ahead of the ache.

And yet, I felt like I was slowly disappearing.

I had everything and nothing at once—a full schedule, a long to-do list, even the occasional applause. But I didn't feel alive. Not really. Because life wasn't moving through me—it was moving around me. I was busy, but not known. I was present, but not felt.

There is a kind of ache that comes from being in the room but not in the hearts of those around you. It's a quiet fading—not because you are unworthy, but because your soul has gone too long without being mirrored back to you.

And that, my love, is not the same as living.

I remember one evening after a long event. The room was full.

Laughter echoed. Music hummed. And still—I felt like I was watching life through glass. I smiled. I answered questions. I played the part. But deep inside, I wondered: *Would it really matter if I weren't here?*

That question didn't shout. It whispered. In small choices. In slow retreats. In skipped plans and muted joy. Not because anyone told me I didn't matter—but because I couldn't feel the echo of my existence in the spaces I was in.

It wasn't until I met with an old friend that something shifted. She looked at me—really looked—and said, *"I've missed your laughter. You make people feel like they belong."*

I had forgotten that.
I had forgotten that I was someone who carried warmth. Who noticed the unseen. Who made room for others.

I had been so busy trying to be useful that I had forgotten I was already valuable.

That was the moment I began rewriting the narrative.
What if I mattered, even when I was quiet?
Even when I wasn't producing or performing?
What if I mattered simply because I carried a presence—a quiet strength—that made others feel safe?

You Are Not Meant to Be Invisible

Some of us grew up learning how to be small.

We were taught that being too loud, too honest, or too emotional made us difficult. So we learned to shrink. To smile through discomfort. To dim our glow when it outshone the room.

But your light, your voice, your unique way of seeing the world— they are not excess. They are your offering to the world.

You are not a background character in someone else's story. You are a whole world.

When you speak, even if your voice trembles, someone hears courage. When you listen, even in silence, someone feels safe. When you stay, even when it's hard, someone begins to believe healing is possible.

You do not need to be loud to be powerful.
You do not need to be celebrated to be significant.
You do not need to be busy to be important.

You just need to keep showing up—fully, and as yourself.

The Difference Only You Can Make

Your presence is the quiet anchor someone else leans on.

I remember a woman who once sat beside me at an event after a hard day and said almost nothing. But her eyes held space. Her stillness made room. Her presence whispered what words could not: *I see you. I'm here.*

I do not remember her job title. I do not remember her achievements. But I remember how she made me feel—*seen.*

Sometimes we think we need to do something extraordinary to matter. But the truth is, your presence, your energy, your essence—are already doing more than you know.

There is a quiet kind of leadership in simply showing up. In noticing what others miss. In offering the kind of softness this world has almost forgotten to value.

There was a time I questioned whether my humble nature added value. I thought I had to perform louder, achieve more, or shine more visibly to matter. But I have come to understand that authentic presence is power.

The way you enter a room. The way you remember what others forget. The way you hold silence without fear—these are not small things. They are the threads that stitch belonging into someone else's life.

You don't need a spotlight to be a guide.
You don't need a platform to hold space.
Your way of being might be the permission someone else needed to finally be themselves.

And that is a gift—the difference only you can make.

So be yourself—fully, tenderly, without apology.
Because the world doesn't need a louder or quieter version of you.
It needs the one that already exists.

Reclaiming the Space That Is Yours

If you have spent years questioning your worth, saying *"I matter"* might feel foreign on your tongue. You may whisper it first. Write it down and stare at it. You may not believe it right away. That's okay. Start there.

Reclaiming space is not about demanding attention. It is about honoring your breath, your body, your being—as worthy.

It is standing a little taller. Saying no when you need to. Letting yourself rest without apology.

I remember once walking into a room full of people who looked nothing like me. Their voices moved fast and sharp, and I felt the urge to shrink—to become smaller, quieter, more agreeable.

But that day, I tried something different.
I placed my feet firmly on the ground. I took a breath.
And I reminded myself: *My presence belongs, even if it doesn't match the room.*

I didn't speak the most. I didn't need to.
But I listened deeply. I shared honestly.
And I left that room not because I had proven anything—
but because I had remained true to myself.

That is reclaiming space.

A New Way to Belong

Imagine yourself as a garden—lush, varied, ever-growing.
Your thoughts, your voice, your presence—these are the soil and seed.

You don't need permission to bloom.
You simply need light and truth.

You get to exist here. You get to bring your whole self to the table.

Wear what feels like you.
Write your story, even if no one has asked for it yet.
Rest. Create. Take up space—not to prove something, but to return to yourself.

Say your name out loud.
Witness your reflection without critique.
Speak to yourself like someone worth loving.
Because you are.

Let This Truth Take Root

You don't belong only when others approve of you.
You belong because you exist.

There is nothing more powerful than a soul fully alive in its truth.
There is nothing more sacred than someone who no longer waits
to be invited—but becomes the invitation.

You do not have to become louder to be heard.
You do not have to become smaller to be accepted.
You simply need to become more of who you already are.

Let your presence be the gift that it already is.
Let your life speak—through your quiet strength, your honest questions, your soft and steady way of holding space.

You are not too much.
You are not too sensitive.
You are not forgotten.

You matter.
And the world is already better because you're in it.

Let that truth take root.
Let it guide you home.

Tools for the Journey:
Return to the Truth of Your Worth

There is a soulful return that begins the moment you stop asking, "Do I matter?" and start gently exploring, "How might I live like I do?" These tools are not a checklist. They are soulful invitations— offered with tenderness, not pressure. They are here to remind you that your presence is not just tolerated; it is needed.

This chapter is for the girl who has crossed borders—geographical, emotional, or spiritual—and found herself in unfamiliar territory. It is also for the part of you that still looks around quietly, wondering, *Is there space for me here?*

You do not need to erase yourself to belong. You do not need to become someone else to be accepted. You need only to remember who you already are—and carry her forward, gently.

Tend to the Inner Child with Compassion

There is a younger version of you who still remembers what it felt like to be overlooked, unheard, or asked to adjust just to be accepted. Begin there. Each morning, ask: *What does she need from me today?* Write her a letter. Let her speak. Let her be seen. You are no longer the child without comfort—you are her return home.

Create Rituals That Anchor You in Worth

When the world around you feels unfamiliar, rituals become reminders that your life still belongs to you. Light a candle. Make tea the way your mother did. Speak your name out loud in a quiet room. Let ordinary actions become sacred touchstones that whisper, *I am still here. I still matter.*

Reclaim the Power of Naming

Your name holds memory, meaning, and identity. Say it fully, without shortening or softening. Teach others how to say it. Write it in your journal. Say it in prayer. Let your name become your compass, your anchor, your affirmation that you are allowed to take up space as you are.

Choose Relationships That Reflect Your Sacredness

You do not have to perform to be loved. You do not have to shrink to stay connected. Choose people who make room for your becoming—who honour your story, even when it's still unfolding. These are your safe places. Let them remind you of your enoughness.

Slow Down and Listen to What Hurts

In the rush to survive, we often bury the ache. But healing begins when you pause to listen. Not to judge or fix—but simply to witness. When you feel that ache, place a hand over your heart and say, *I hear you. I am staying.*

Build a Sense of Safety Through the Senses

Safety is not something you think—it's something you feel. Wrap yourself in warmth. Play familiar music. Cook food that smells like childhood. Let your five senses remind you that even in unfamiliar places, you can still create peace.

Write Yourself Back Into the Story

When trauma or change interrupts the storyline of who you thought you were, writing can help you return. Try this prompt: *If I fully believed I mattered, how would I move through today?* Let your words become your pathway back to truth—not polished, but real.

Practice Boundaries as Acts of Self-Honour

Boundaries are not walls. They are bridges between you and your deepest truth. Start small: take time for yourself, say no without apology, or pause before saying yes. These are sacred ways of saying: *My peace matters, too.*

Regulate by Returning to Presence

You do not need to be calm all the time. But you do deserve to feel supported inside your own skin. When the world feels loud, ground yourself with touch: a hand to your chest, your feet on the floor. Speak softly to yourself: *I am here. I am safe. I belong.*

Let Joy Be a Quiet Rebellion

Joy is not the absence of hardship—it is the breath that rises anyway. Seek out what makes you smile: dancing alone, laughing with a friend, feeling sunlight on your face. Let joy be your declaration that your life is still yours to live.

These tools are not tasks. They are gentle companions. Let them rise and return like breath—consistent, forgiving, and entirely yours.

Because belonging is not something the world grants you.
It is something you begin to feel when you start honoring yourself again.
You matter, beloved.
Not because you've proven it.
But because you are here.

CHAPTER 3

To the Girl Who's the Adult in Her Home —

You have carried too much, too soon.

Some of us didn't just feel unseen. We carried entire homes on our backs, while still being called children; my dear brave one,

I want to begin by gently naming what you may have carried for far too long: life can be painfully unfair. Sometimes, the weight you hold is not of your own making, yet you bear it with quiet strength and unwavering presence. I cannot explain why some are born into shelter and others into storms—but what I know, in the marrow of my being, is this: you should have been held. You should have been protected. You should have been cherished, simply because you are you.

You should have been allowed to be a child.
But instead, life asked you to grow up too fast.
And you did—because you are strong, and because you had no other choice.

You learned how to translate chaos into calm. You became the voice of reason when adults lost theirs. You carried burdens your shoulders were never meant to bear. You wiped away your own tears and still had space to comfort others. Maybe you made meals when you were too young to reach the stove. Maybe you kept the peace while everything around you was falling apart.

You grew into someone who held it all together—and sometimes, that meant losing pieces of yourself along the way.

I want you to know I see you. Not just for what you've done, but for what you've lost. The innocence. The ease. The right to be carefree. You deserved more. And yet, even with all that has been asked of you, you have remained tender. You still love. You still hope. That is no small miracle.

It's okay if you are tired.
It's okay if you feel angry.
It's okay if you long for someone to say,
"You don't have to do this alone anymore."

Let this be that moment.

You do not have to hold everything. Not forever. You do not have to keep proving your strength by how well you carry what breaks you. You are allowed to set it down now. You are allowed to ask for help. You are allowed to be soft.

You are not broken for feeling overwhelmed.
You are not weak for wanting rest.
You are not selfish for needing something just for you.

There is a little girl inside you still waiting to be told: *You've done enough. You get to come home now.*

So let these words be your invitation.
Take off the armor. Let your shoulders drop. Let yourself cry if you need to. Let someone hold you, even if it's just these words for now.

You don't have to earn love by holding it all together.
You already are love. You already are worthy.

You are not alone, precious one. And you never were.

With deep tenderness,
The one who remembers your softness

Life Lesson:
You Have Carried Too Much, Too Soon

Some of us grow up with backpacks far too heavy for our years—ones filled with unpaid bills, parentified roles, and the quiet maturity forged in the fires of displacement, hunger, or survival. These are the invisible weights carried by too many girls around the world. The expectations that leave no room for childhood. If this is your story, I want you to know: you are not forgotten.

This chapter is for the girl who became the adult too early. Who translated chaos into calm. Who traded play for peacekeeping. Whose quiet endurance held the roof up while no one noticed. I know her, because I was her.

Some moments live so deeply in the body they no longer feel like memory—they feel like marrow. I remember being eleven, just after the world around us collapsed into conflict and genocide, holding my younger sibling's hand while trying not to cry. My parents were focused on keeping us alive, and I—still a child—stepped into the cracks where safety had fallen away. There was no room for fear or tears. Only function. Only survival.

When I became a refugee, the rituals of girlhood were replaced with the urgency of staying alive. Washing clothes. Cooking meals. Walking ten kilometers for water. Listening for danger. I couldn't afford to be afraid for long—I had to adapt. And when we resettled, I carried all of that with me. I got us to school. I translated every document, every appointment. I learned to navigate systems I had never chosen, not for myself, but for all of us. I wasn't just surviving. I was carrying.

Maybe your story is different. Maybe it didn't involve war or displacement. Maybe it meant calming a parent's emotions, raising your siblings, or becoming the adult in a house that forgot you were still a child. Different setting, same ache.

You didn't have time to learn your favorite color, your rhythm, your joy. You were too busy holding everything together.

And the trouble with growing up too fast is this: the world begins to see you as capable—but not as human. As strong—but not as someone who still longs to be held. Over time, you begin to measure your worth by how much you can carry. You think: *If I stay strong, maybe someone will stay. If I keep helping, maybe nothing else will break.*

But the truth is—no child should have to earn their safety. And no grown woman should have to prove she's still worthy of care.

Let's pause here. Breathe.
There is a child within you still waiting to hear: *I see you. I know it was hard. I am so proud of you.*

Learning to Parent Yourself with Tenderness

For those of us who grew up too soon, care can feel foreign. Receiving kindness can feel like a threat. Rest can feel like failure.

But what if we chose, gently and without urgency, to explore a different way? A way that softens around the wounds. A way that reminds us: we, too, are worthy of the compassion we've always given to others.

Think about how you've shown up for others—the meals, the translations, the reassurances. Now imagine offering that same devotion inward.

This is not selfish. It is sacred. It is healing.

Parenting yourself means asking: *What do I need right now?* And trusting that the answer matters. It means choosing softness without guilt. It means letting go of the lie that your value depends on how well you hold it all together.

When I first tried this, it felt unfamiliar. I didn't even know what brought me joy. I had spent so long becoming what others needed, I forgot how to listen inward. But slowly, I returned.

I began lighting a candle before bed and whispering,
You're safe now.
I wrote notes to the child I had been: *You don't have to earn love today.*
I sought therapy—not to be fixed, but to remember that softness is not weakness.

Each act, however small, became a way home.

Honoring the Grief of Lost Childhood

One of the hardest parts of healing is grieving what was never given. No birthday candles. No one to tuck you in. No room to fall apart.

And that grief is real. It is valid.

Sometimes we try to bypass grief by saying, *It made me strong.* And yes, maybe it did. But it also made you tired.

You are allowed to name what you missed.
You are allowed to cry for what was taken.
You are allowed to want more.

Grief does not make you ungrateful.
It makes you honest. And honesty is where healing begins.

You Are Not Just What You've Survived

You are not just a fixer, a helper, a soldier in someone else's war. You are a soul with longings. A heart that still dreams. A person with a story beyond what you've done for others.

Who are you when no one is asking you to carry?
What makes you laugh without guilt?
What brings you peace when no one is watching?

Your life is not a checklist.
It is a song. And even if the first verses began in pain, you are allowed to write a new chorus.

Becoming the Safe Place You Always Needed

You may never receive the apology you deserved. You may never get back the childhood you lost. But you can become the safe place you always needed.

You can build a life that whispers: *You are allowed to rest here.*

It begins with gentleness.
With not pushing past exhaustion.
With saying no.
With remembering that you matter—even when you're not carrying the world.

You have carried too much, too soon.
But now, love, it is your turn to be carried.

Let the weight fall.
Let your breath deepen.
Let your story shift.

You have not failed.
You have survived.

And now—*now you get to live.*

Tools for the Journey:
Let This Be a Beginning

Starting over is not a sign of failure. It is an act of courage—a quiet, soulful declaration that you still believe in something more. These tools are not blueprints for perfection. They are gentle companions for the days when your hope feels fragile and your past feels too close.

This chapter is for the girl who has carried too much, too early. The one who became strong out of necessity. The one who is now learning to soften—not because she is weak, but because she is finally safe enough to rest.

You do not need to reinvent yourself to begin again. You need only to return to what has always been true: your softness is sacred. Your needs are valid. Your restart is not a regression—it is a return.

Begin with Gentle Self-Recognition

Before you move forward, pause to see the girl who kept going. The one who held the pieces when no one else did. The one who made it through without being seen. Whisper to her now: *I see you. I honour you. You did not deserve to carry it all alone.*

Name the Tenderness You Needed

So much of healing begins with naming—not just what happened, but what was missing. Name the gentleness you craved. The safety you never had. The care you were denied. This is not about blame. It is about truth-telling. And truth-telling is sacred ground.

Let Grief Have Its Place

Grief is not just for loss. It is for the childhood you did not get to live. It is for the joy you had to postpone. Let the ache rise. Let the tears come. Sit with your sorrow as if it belongs—because it does. Healing makes room for what hurts.

Reclaim the Right to Rest

If you were taught that rest was lazy or selfish, you may still feel guilt when you pause. But rest is not indulgent—it is holy. Especially for those who never had permission to stop. Lay down. Breathe. Say aloud: *This moment belongs to me.*

Build Routines That Centre Your Wholeness

A rhythm that honours you is not glamorous—it is grounding. Begin with what steadies you: a warm bowl of food, a bedtime ritual, a moment of stillness before dawn. These are not habits. They are soul-anchors.

Let Softness Redefine Strength

Strength is not the absence of pain. It is the willingness to be seen in your tenderness. Let your power include your vulnerability. Let your bravery sound like *"I need help."* Let softness be your revolution.

Practice Receiving Without Apology

You have always known how to give. Now, learn how to receive. Accept kindness without shrinking. Let someone carry something for you. Being held does not make you weak—it makes you human.

Speak the Truth You Silenced

If your survival depended on staying quiet, your voice may still feel dangerous. But you are not in danger now. Practice telling the truth, even if your voice trembles. Start with a journal. A prayer. A trusted friend. You deserve to speak and still be safe.

Soften the Voice Within

You have lived long enough with criticism disguised as protection. Begin rewriting the script: *I did my best. I am learning. I am lovable as I am.* Let the voice inside you sound like the friend you always needed.

Ask for Support Without Shame

You were never meant to do this alone. Reach out—to a therapist, a mentor, a sister, a stranger who understands. Support is not dependence. It is a bridge back to belonging. Let yourself be held.

These are not tools you must master. They are practices that live with you, in your breath, in your being, in your remembering.

Some days, you will forget them. That is okay. You can return. Again and again.

Because healing from a childhood of too much, too soon is not about becoming someone new.

It is about giving the girl who survived a life where she no longer has to.

And if you're carrying dreams like pebbles in your pocket, unsure if they're still allowed to shine—Let this be your permission.

You are allowed to want more. You are allowed to rest. You are allowed to begin again. You are not broken. You are building something new—from the wisdom of your roots.

Let This Be the Beginning

Healing from a childhood of too much, too soon is not about reaching perfection. It is about learning to honour the girl who survived—and gently offering her a life where she no longer has to. It is about returning, again and again, to the parts of you that had to grow up quickly, and softly reminding them: it is safe to rest now.

You are not behind. You are not broken. You are learning how to give yourself what you never received.

There may still be days when the old weight returns. When you feel the ache of responsibility, the urge to hold it all together. When your body remembers before your mind catches up. That is okay. You are allowed to pause. You are allowed to soften. You are allowed to begin again.

Let these tools be your compass—not a cure, but a collection of sacred reminders. Let them guide you not just toward resilience, but toward tenderness. Toward joy. Toward breath.

May you learn to mother yourself with the same fierce grace you once gave to others. May you find spaces where your laughter rings without guilt, and your tears are welcomed without shame. May you build a home within yourself that says, every single day: You belong here. You matter here. You are safe here.

And above all, may you remember this:

You are no longer just surviving.
You are becoming.

Becoming whole.
Becoming free.
Becoming the girl who no longer has to carry it all alone.

You have done enough.
Now, beloved one—
Let yourself be held.

From One Heart to Another —
Trust the Timing of your Bloom *Letter from a champion*

Dear Girl,

If I could sit across from you now, I would take your hand, look you in the eye, and say this gently but firmly: You are enough. You are loved. You are full of possibility. You carry a light that is entirely your own—and the world needs it, even if it hasn't been fully seen yet.

You don't need to have it all figured out. What you do need is a spark—a curiosity, a passion, a sense that there's something within you worth exploring. Follow that. Even if it seems impractical. Even if others don't understand. That spark is your inner genius.

I spent much of my life following the path laid out for me—excelling in school, earning a Ph.D. in electrical engineering, becoming a senior scientist at the Department of National Defence, and an adjunct professor at Carleton University. On paper, everything looked perfect.

But something was missing. That something was passion.

Through a friend, I discovered real estate investment as a side interest. It began as a hobby—then became a calling. I felt alive and fulfilled helping people make important life decisions and generate wealth through real estate. I realized I was a people person, and my real strength was connecting with people.

At the age of 48, I made a leap that surprised everyone: I left my secure government job and launched my real estate business.

People questioned my choice.

"Wasn't this a waste of your Ph.D.?"
"Are you sure about giving up job security and a pension?"

But I had finally discovered something precious—something that had been quietly waiting inside me all along: passion.

It wasn't an easy decision. I had spent years doing what I thought I was supposed to do: choosing stability and seeking approval. But deep down, I always felt a quiet tug, a longing to do something more aligned with who I really was.

That's why I am writing to you now. I want to tell you—you don't have to wait until midlife to listen to yourself. You don't need to silence your curiosity, or, squeeze yourself into a version of success that doesn't feel right. I made the leap late, but you can start tuning in earlier. Your life is yours to design.

And here's what I've come to believe—truths I wish I had known earlier, and that I now want to share with you, so you feel empowered to walk your own path with confidence and grace:

1. Follow your passion—it is your inner genius.

Passion is not a luxury. It's not something reserved for artists or dreamers. It's your compass, your power source, your truth. It reveals what makes you come alive—and when you follow it, you unlock your unique gift to the world. That is your genius.

It may arrive as a whisper or a tug. It may come late in life, as it did for me. But when it does, honor it, nurture it, because it will guide you home to yourself.

2. Grow your confidence—one choice at a time.

I was once an A+ student. I did what I was told. I followed the rules. I cared deeply about what others thought. But confidence doesn't come from approval. It comes from action. From choosing yourself.

I'm still learning to speak to myself kindly: You're doing your best. Keep going.

I invite you to do the same.

3. You don't need to be perfect to be loved.

This may be the most important lesson of all:

You are lovable as you are.

You don't need flawless skin, straight As, or constant praise.

You don't need to shrink or perform to be accepted.

For years, I chased perfection—trying to be everything to everyone. But I've learned this: we are all flawed and fallible human beings. And we are worthy anyway.

So speak to yourself the way you would to a dear friend—with kindness, understanding, and forgiveness. Let yourself be messy, human, evolving. That's where the beauty lives.

4. Seek mentors—and become one.

My journey has been guided by others—people who opened doors, shared wisdom, and believed in me. My father's motto was, "Find joy in helping others." That has become my compass.

Today, I lead a multicultural real estate company with the culture "Care, Give, Serve." We support charities. We host community events. Why? Because success is sweeter when shared. I want to create the kind of support I once needed.

So if you're ever unsure, don't stay silent. Ask for guidance. Reach out. And one day, when you can—reach back.

Forging your path won't always be easy. There will be doubt, detours, and days that feel like failure. But if you keep walking—step by step—you'll discover something powerful:

You own your life!

For years, I let others choose for me. I followed the safe road. But today, I make my own decisions. I live by design, not by default. And I wake up every morning excited to help others do the same.

If no one's told you yet—you have the right to dream your own dreams.

You have the power to create something new, something uniquely yours!

To end, I want to share a poem I wrote:

Let's Dance! ---By Helen Tang

When the sun rises,

Let's dance!

Shake every muscle,

Celebrate a new day to come!

When the sun sets,

Let's dance!

Throw all worries,

Free your soul!

When the rain falls,

Let's dance!

Soak up in happiness,

Cheer for rainbow!

When the winter comes,

Let's dance!

Warm up every fiber,

Spring is around the corner!

Whatever season you're in, keep dancing.

Keep listening. Keep becoming.

Because…

You are enough. I am enough. We are enough.

I believe in you.

I'll be cheering for you.

And the best is yet to come.

With all my love,

Helen

PART II

Be Brave: Face What Hurt You

Your pain has a story. Your story holds power.

A courageous exploration of what happened to you, how it shaped you, and how facing it is the beginning of reclaiming your life.

There comes a moment in every healing journey when we stop running—and instead, turn gently toward the places that ache. Not to relive them. Not to blame. But to understand. To say with steady compassion: *Yes, this happened. And yes, it mattered.*

Pain does not dissolve in silence. When unspoken, it burrows deep and resurfaces in quieter forms—perfectionism, people-pleasing, burnout, anxiety, shame. It begins to shape our decisions, our self-image, our capacity to feel safe in the world. But when we shine light on those early wounds—with tenderness and truth—something begins to soften. We free the parts of ourselves that got frozen in survival. We begin to breathe again.

This part of your journey asks for courage—not the kind that charges ahead with armor, but the kind that sits beside the younger version of you and says: *I am here now. You are not alone.*

Here, we meet the girl who was silenced, dismissed, hurt, overlooked. We no longer ask her to be quiet. We offer her our full presence. We bear witness. We listen without rushing her forward. We begin to understand not just what happened to her, but how she carried it. How she adapted. How she made herself small or loud or invisible to stay safe.

To face the past is not to stay in it. It is to reclaim the narrative. To say: *This shaped me—but it does not get to define me anymore.* It is to hold space for grief, for rage, for confusion—and also for clarity, for courage, and for rebirth.

This section is an invitation to be brave. Not perfect. Not healed. Just brave enough to be present. Brave enough to feel what you've been carrying. Brave enough to tell the truth, softly and in your own time.

Because every time you choose truth over silence, you become a little more free. And every step you take toward your own healing makes it safer for someone else to take theirs.

Let this be the part where you begin to see your pain not as a flaw to hide, but as a doorway to wholeness. Let this be where shame loosens its grip. Where your tenderness returns. Where your story, just as it is, begins to lead you home.

You are allowed to feel it all.
You are allowed to take your time.
You are allowed to begin again.

Let's begin.

CHAPTER 4

To the One Surviving Something No One Knows About —

You are not alone in your silence.

You have been carrying something heavy for so long—and yet you walk through the world as if it weighs nothing. You smile when it hurts. You show up even when your heart is breaking. And sometimes, you sit quietly in a crowded room, holding stories that no one else knows, wondering if anyone would still love you if they ever heard the truth.

I want you to know: You are not alone.

The things you've survived—the fear, the confusion, the moments that changed you—are not reflections of your worth. They are reminders of your resilience. Of your tenderness. Of how deeply you feel, even when the world hasn't felt kind.

You do not need to justify your pain. You do not need permission to name it. The fact that you have carried all of this and are still here? That matters. **You matter.**

Some hurts live in silence. Some wounds never bleed, but they shape the way you breathe, the way you trust, the way you hold yourself at night. Just because no one saw what happened doesn't mean it didn't leave a mark. Just because you kept going doesn't mean it didn't cost you something.

You've been surviving. Quietly. Fiercely.

And that survival is sacred. It doesn't need to be explained. It only needs to be honored.

You don't have to keep pretending. Not here. Not with me.

Let your shoulders drop. Let your breath slow. Let yourself cry if you need to. Because love, there is nothing wrong with you. What happened to you was never your fault.

And even though you've learned how to be strong, you are allowed to be soft now, too.

Your story is not shameful. It is sacred. It is yours.

One day, when you're ready, you will speak it. Not because you owe it to anyone, but because you'll feel free enough to no longer carry it alone.

And that story—your story—will be the key that unlocks healing for someone else.

But for now, just rest in this truth: You are not alone. You are not invisible. And you are deeply, deeply loved.

With all my heart,
The one who sees you

Life Lesson:
When Silence Is a Survival Strategy

There are many ways we learn to survive. Some run. Others freeze. Some of us learn to smile so beautifully that no one ever asks what is wrong. And some—like you—learn to stay quiet. Not because you do not want to speak, but because your voice never felt safe enough to land. Silence, then, becomes more than absence—it becomes armor.

When we carry pain that no one knows about, it is not because we want to be invisible. It is because, somewhere along the way, we were taught that visibility could cost us safety, connection, or even love. So we read the room. We shrink our needs. We manage everyone else's comfort. We become expert caretakers—masters at hiding our pain. And we do all of it with a tenderness so deep that the world often misses the ache behind our resilience.

I remember the first time I realized I was holding immense fear. I was ten. I had lived through something terrifying—though I did not have the words to name it. Nothing visible had harmed me, but my body understood something I could not explain. My chest tightened. My throat closed. I froze—not because I wanted to, but because it felt like the only way to stay safe. That silence became my shelter. Not by choice, but by instinct.

Years later, I met girls who had survived so much more—abuse, war, forced marriage, violence, silencing by fear, culture, or danger. And yet, the same quiet lived in their eyes. The same knowing. The same survival. We shared no words, but we shared everything.

What I have come to understand now—with gentleness and time—is this: what we carry in silence is not shameful. It is sacred. It is the wisdom of the body protecting itself. Your silence is not a flaw. It is an intelligent, instinctive act of preservation. But the same silence that kept you safe can also keep you stuck—if you never allow yourself to be seen.

So here is a gentle invitation—not a command, not an expectation. Just a soft place to begin:

What if your voice was never dangerous? What if it is the very thing that could set you free?

When we begin to name our pain, even quietly—even shakily—we shift the story from "This happened to me, and I must hide it," to "This happened to me, and I am still worthy of love." That shift is everything. That is how healing begins.

Start small. Write a letter you never send or journal. Speak your truth when no one is listening. Whisper it into the wind, if you must. What matters most is that *you* hear it. Not for them. For you.

You survived. You adapted. You endured. And now, beloved, you get to reclaim your voice.

You Are Not to Blame

If you are carrying pain you have never shared—especially pain caused by someone else—it is easy to start internalizing the blame. You might think, *Maybe I let it happen. Maybe I could have stopped it.* Or you might wonder why you were born into hardship—why you've had to carry so much you never chose.

Whether you grew up in a war zone, lived through poverty, or bore the weight of injustice far too young, know this: your circumstances were never a reflection of your worth. They reflect a world that needs to be more just, more loving, and more whole. Your survival is a quiet act of revolution against that brokenness.

What happened to you was not your fault.

I know that may be hard to believe—especially if no one has ever said it to you before. But please hear this now: You did not deserve the pain you lived through. None of us do. We may come from different places. We may walk different roads. But this truth holds for us all: **You are not to blame for the harm that was done to you.**

You are not broken. You were broken open. And in that opening, the light began to rise.

There is something sacred about the girl who knows what it means to hurt—and still chooses love.

Something powerful about the one who walks through the world with her heart open, even after it was shattered.

What to Do When the Pain Returns

Even after naming your pain, there will be days when it returns. In memories. In sensations. In shadows that feel too familiar.

This does not mean you are failing. It means you are healing.

The body holds memory longer than the mind. A voice, a scent, a hallway can awaken what you thought was gone. And in those moments, be gentle. Place a hand over your heart. Breathe slowly. Speak to yourself the way you wish someone had spoken to you:

You are not back there. You are here.
You are safe. You are seen. Here, you are allowed to rest.

A Quiet Strength

Some of the bravest people I have ever known do not speak loudly.

They simply keep going—even when no one knows what they are carrying.

So to the girl who is surviving something no one knows about—I hope you know: You are not invisible. You are not alone. You matter. Your story matters. Your healing matters.

You do not need to have the perfect words. You do not need to be ready to tell the story. You just need to begin. And I am so grateful that you are here, as you read this I am grateful that we are on this journey together, I am proud of you for breathing through this, for simply staying because i whileheately believe that you are a gift and you are a light. Your silence was never emptiness.

It was the sound of survival.

Tools for the Journey:
When You Are Ready to Face What Hurt

There is a quiet kind of bravery that comes not from fighting—but from facing. From turning toward the ache instead of away. From asking, not "Why me?" but "What now?" These tools are offered not as tasks, but as invitations.

Not to fix what happened.
But to befriend the one who survived it.

This chapter is for the girl who carries stories no one knows. For the woman who has held herself together for far too long. For the soul who has whispered, "It did happen," and is now learning to speak the truth—not as a weapon, but as a path to freedom.

You do not need to rush. You only need to begin.

Name What Has Lived in Silence

Begin with what feels honest—not what sounds polished. You do not have to retell the whole story at once. Try simple truths: *"This still hurts." "I do not know how to feel safe."* Naming your truth, even in fragments, is how you make room for it to heal.

Create an Anchor of Safety Before You Begin

Healing does not happen in chaos—it happens in the presence of calm. Choose a space that feels steady. Light a candle. Breathe with intention. Wrap yourself in a warm shawl. Let your body know: *We are safe now. We can tell the truth.*

Find Witnesses Who Honour, Not Invalidate

Not everyone is meant to hear your story. Choose those who listen with their heart, not their assumptions. Whether a therapist, a mentor, a trusted friend, or the pages of a journal—your truth deserves to be held, not questioned.

Reparent the Child Who Thought It Was Her Fault

Speak gently to the girl inside you. Tell her what no one did: *"You were never too much." "It was never your fault." "You are safe with me now."* Let her know you're here to protect her the way no one did before.

Practice Truth-Telling Without Performing

You do not owe your pain to anyone. But you do deserve to stop hiding it from yourself. Write it down. Whisper it in the dark. Say it in prayer. Not to prove anything, but to remind yourself: *I am still here. My story matters.*

Let the Body Guide the Healing, Too

Trauma often teaches us to abandon the body. Begin by returning with kindness. Ground your feet. Place a hand on your belly. Stretch slowly. Breathe deeply. Let your body feel your presence— not as punishment, but as peace.

Stay Gentle with the Waves

Some days the pain may rush back like a tide. You might feel raw, unsure, or angry. That does not mean you are broken. It means you are healing. Healing is not linear—it is layered. Let yourself feel, and let yourself rest.

Use Rituals as Healing Language

Rituals are not luxury. They are language—telling your nervous system that you are safe to be human. Try holding your own hand before sleep. Repeat a phrase that soothes you. Burn something symbolic of what you are ready to release. These acts speak louder than words to the parts of you still afraid.

Let the Truth Be Enough—Even in a Whisper

You do not need to shout to be heard. You do not need to share everything to be seen. Begin with what feels possible. And when the voice of shame grows loud, return to this: *I am telling my story not to blame, but to be free.*

You are not alone in your remembering.
And you never were.

Each word you write, each truth you name, each tear you allow to fall is a thread weaving you back to yourself.

This is not weakness.
This is power—the kind the world cannot measure.

So speak, love. Whisper if you must.
You are not too late.
You are not too much.
You are not broken.

You are becoming free.

CHAPTER 5

To the One Who Was Bullied Today —

You are more than their words.

I am so sorry they hurt you.

Those words—sharp like glass, thrown carelessly like they meant nothing—cut deeper than anyone can see. You carry the sting in silence, maybe even in shame, wondering if something about you invited the cruelty. Let me tell you now: it didn't.

You did not deserve to be hurt. You are not the problem. Their words say more about their pain than your worth.

I know it is hard to believe when the echo of their voices is louder than your own. But just because they couldn't see your light doesn't mean it isn't shining. Just because they made you feel small doesn't mean you are.

You matter. Right now. As you are. Not when you've changed. Not when you've toughened up. Not when you are finally "enough" for them. You are enough already.

What they said about you—whatever they mocked, laughed at, or dismissed—does not get to define you. You are so much more than the way they treated you. Their cruelty cannot dim the truth of who you are: you are loved. You are needed. You are becoming someone powerful and tender and true.

And while they were busy trying to tear you down, you were quietly learning how to rise.

Please do not turn their pain into your belief system. Do not carry their voices into your future. Carry your own.

The one that whispers, *"I am still here. And I still believe in myself."*

Because you are still here. And that matters.

You are not what they said. You are what you choose to believe about yourself. And I hope you believe this: you are beautiful. You are strong. You are worth defending.

Even on the days you feel fragile, you are not broken. You are building something that cannot be shaken—your sense of self.

Hold on to that. And know this:
You are not alone. You are seen. And your story is not over.

With all my heart,
Someone who sees your light

Life Lesson:
When Words Wound

Words can feel like walls. Like wounds. Like weights. And when they are aimed at you—mocking your name, your body, your story—they do not just bruise the surface. They settle into the softest parts of you, echoing until your inner voice begins to sound like theirs.

If you have been bullied, you already know: it is not just about what was said. It is about the silence that follows. The echo. The doubt. The way those voices travel into the corners of your mind and begin to reshape how you see yourself.

Sometimes, it starts young—on the playground, in the lunch line, behind a screen, or in front of a crowd. And when it continues, the world, not knowing what to do, often tells you to "just ignore it" or "be the bigger person."

But here is what the world forgets: bullying is not just a bad day. It is a slow unraveling of your safety. A message, repeated and cruel, that says you are too much, or not enough, or somehow unworthy of love.

And yet—here you are. Still standing. Still soft. Still showing up.

That is not weakness. That is courage of the highest kind.

When the Mirror Changes

I still remember the first time I looked in the mirror and didn't recognize myself.

I was thirteen. New to a school in a country where I didn't yet speak the language. I brought lunch from home—a warm, fragrant dish my grandmother had taught me to make. It smelled of turmeric, safety, and home. But in the cafeteria, it became a target.

I heard the laughter before I saw the stares. Heard someone mimic my accent. Saw someone wrinkle their nose. Someone said I looked like I didn't belong. And in that moment, I started to believe them.

That is what bullying does. It doesn't just hurt—it distorts. It whispers: *Be smaller. Quieter. Less. Hide what makes you different. Shrink until you disappear.*

But you, love, were never meant to disappear.
You were meant to take up space.

For the Girl Anywhere in the World

If you are reading this from a city filled with bright lights, from a refugee camp beneath a wide, dusty sky, or from a village where clean water is still a hope—not a guarantee—know this: this message is for you.

You may be carrying layers of pain. You may be bullied not only for how you look or speak, but for who your family is, what you believe, or the skin you are in. In some places, girls are punished for being smart, for showing joy, for daring to have a voice. In others, you are teased for not fitting into someone else's version of "enough." Sometimes, your difference becomes your danger.

But that difference? That is where your light lives.

You are not what they said.

You are the lullabies your mother hummed when the world felt too loud. You are the hope your ancestors carried in their bones. You are what remains when cruelty fades and truth takes root.

Reclaiming Your Voice

When someone tries to erase you with their words, the most radical thing you can do is stay visible. You do not need to shout to reclaim your power. You simply need to stop apologizing for being real.

That might look like writing your truth in a notebook no one else reads. Wearing the color that makes you feel strong. Saying no to friendships that leave you feeling smaller. Saying yes to standing taller when everything in you wants to curl in.

Each act is a quiet declaration: *I am still here. I deserve to be.*

When I began writing my truths—shaky at first, small at first—I began coming home to myself. One day I wrote, *They do not get to tell the story of me.* And from there, I started writing the version I wanted to believe. Over time, my voice grew louder than theirs.

When the Pain Comes Back

Even years later, bullying can echo. You might walk into a room and feel that old shame rise up. You might hear someone laugh and wonder, *Are they laughing at me?*

This is not weakness. It is memory. And memory does not mean you are broken—it means you are healing.

When that ache returns, pause. Breathe. Place your hand over your heart and say gently:

I am not back there. I am here now. I am safe.

Becoming the Safe Place You Always Needed

Maybe no one stood up for you. Maybe a teacher looked away. Maybe a parent didn't see the quiet collapse behind your smile.

You deserved more.

But now, you get to become that safe place for yourself.

You can look in the mirror and say, *I believe you.*
You can choose people who speak your name with respect.
You can protect your peace.

And if you have not yet found someone who makes you feel safe,
you can be that someone—for yourself, and for someone else.

Because your tenderness is not a weakness. It is wisdom.
Your awareness is not a burden. It is leadership.
And leaders who have known pain often lead with compassion.

A Future They Cannot Take From You

The most powerful response to cruelty is not revenge.
It is becoming someone so grounded in truth that nothing unkind
can shake you.

You do not need to prove your worth.
You do not need their apology or approval.
You simply need to keep walking forward.

The words they threw at you?
They do not belong to you.

Give them back.
And walk with your own:

"I am enough."
"I matter."
"I am still here."

Reflections: Questions to Ask Yourself

- What moment still lingers from when someone tried to make you feel small?

- What truth can you speak to that moment now?

- What parts of yourself have you hidden because of someone else's words?

- What would it mean to give those parts space again?

- If you could write a letter to your younger self on the day you were bullied, what would you say?

You Are Still Becoming

You are not broken because you were bullied.
You are breaking open. And inside that opening is strength.

Your light is not gone—it has just been waiting.
Waiting for the moment you remember: *Their words are not more powerful than my story.*

And that moment can be now.

Speak gently to yourself.
Wrap your arms around the parts of you that still flinch.
Say what no one else did:

"You're okay."
"You're good."
"You're worthy."

And then—rise.

You are more than their words. You always were.
You're not finished yet.
You are still becoming.
And that becoming is beautiful.

Tools for the Journey:
Heal the Invisible Wounds of Words

There is a part of healing that lives quietly beneath the surface. It does not leave scars you can point to. It leaves imprints in the way you breathe, brace, and belong. When someone bullies you, it is not just the words that wound—it is the message they plant inside you. This section is for that quiet part of you still carrying the echoes. These tools are not tasks. They are small returns to yourself—sacred acts of remembering that you were never what they said. You are who you choose to become.

Begin with the Breath That Grounds You

Your breath is the first thing fear steals—and the first thing healing can restore. When you feel tension rise or memories return, place one hand on your heart, the other on your belly. Inhale slowly for four counts. Hold for four. Exhale for six. Repeat. This gentle rhythm signals to your body: I am safe now. You do not have to brace. You are home.

Name What Was Said—and What It Stole

Bullying often teaches silence. But healing invites you to name what happened. Not for revenge, but for release. Write down the words that still echo in your mind. Then name how they made you feel—small, ashamed, invisible. Naming is not reliving. It is reclaiming your voice from the places it was lost.

Reclaim the Voice That Was Shamed Into Silence

Bullies do not just insult you—they rewrite your inner narrative. You begin to question your beauty, your kindness, your strength. But those were not your words. They were projections of someone else's pain. Start with one truth: *I am allowed to take up space. I am not what they said—I am who I choose to become.* Let your voice rise louder than their echoes.

Let Movement Speak What Words Cannot

Not all pain speaks in language. Sometimes it speaks in stillness, tightness, or tears. Let your body move in ways that feel freeing. Dance. Walk. Stretch. Cry. Let your limbs tell the story your voice has not yet spoken. Healing lives in the spaces where your body finally feels safe enough to exhale.

Create Spaces That Feel Like Shelter

Safety is not a luxury—it is a necessity for healing. Ask yourself: *Where does my soul feel most held?* It could be a room, a playlist, a person, or even your journal. Build those sanctuaries with intention. Let them become places where your nervous system remembers peace, and your spirit remembers joy.

Speak to the Inner Girl Who Was Hurt

Even if you are grown, a younger you still carries the sting of laughter that cut too deep or words that made you question your worth. Close your eyes and speak to her: *You did not deserve that. It was never your fault. You were always worthy of love.* Let her know she is safe with you now. You are the comfort she waited for.

Let Beauty Be a Daily Act of Resistance

Healing is not only about what you survived—it is also about what you allow yourself to enjoy. Sip something warm. Watch the sky change. Plant something and watch it grow. Let joy become your quiet rebellion. Let beauty remind you that your story is still unfolding—and there is so much good left to receive.

Honor Your Healing Without a Deadline

Some days will be tender. Some memories may resurface when you least expect them. That does not mean you are broken. It means you are human. Healing is not about speed. It is about presence. Let yourself take time. Let yourself be soft. Let yourself be free from the pressure to be "over it." You are allowed to heal at your own pace.

You were never meant to carry someone else's cruelty as if it were the truth.
You are not what they said.
You are not broken.
You are becoming.
And every step you take back to yourself is sacred.

CHAPTER 6

To the Girl Starting Over (Again) —

Even restarts carry wisdom from your roots.

I know this is not your first time beginning again.

You have rebuilt before—after heartbreak, after disappointment, after walking away from places and people that once felt like home. Maybe you're stepping into a new city. Or learning to speak a new language. Maybe you're letting go of a relationship that left too many invisible bruises on your spirit. Or maybe you're simply waking up each day, trying to believe that something better is still possible.

Whatever your beginning looks like, I want you to know this: just because you are starting over again does not mean you failed. It means you are still becoming.

Sometimes life strips us bare—not to punish us, but to reveal the strength we forgot we carried. And sometimes, starting over is not about forgetting the past, but about standing with it and gently saying, *I deserve more than this pain.*

Even if it feels like you are standing at the edge of the unknown, you are not empty. You are full of everything that has carried you here—the quiet courage, the resilience threaded into your bones, the nights you held yourself together when no one knew you were unraveling.

You are not beginning from nothing.
You are beginning from wisdom.

You do not have to rush. You do not have to have it all figured out.
You only need to keep breathing—and trust that the version of
you being born through this breaking is rooted in something true.

You have always been brave. But maybe this time, your bravery
looks different. Maybe it looks like resting. Asking for help.
Saying no. Saying yes to small joys, even before everything is
perfect. Maybe it looks like forgiving yourself. Like trusting joy
again before you are sure it is safe.

Starting over is not weakness. It is a sacred invitation. To choose
again. To return to what matters. To remember who you are
beneath the grief and the noise.

And that girl—the one still here, still trying, still tender?

She is not broken. She is wisdom wrapped in skin. She is strength
with a quiet voice. She is becoming, again.

You are not behind. You are not lost.
You are on your way.

And love—Even restarts bloom from roots that run deep.

Life Lesson:
When Restarts Become Your Rhythm

There are seasons in life that do not arrive with warning signs or fanfare. They come quietly—or crash in suddenly—leaving you standing in the ruins of what used to be: a plan, a dream, a home. You find yourself asking, *How did I end up here again?*

Starting over is something many of us come to know intimately. Whether it is moving countries, losing family, ending a relationship, or waking up to realize that the life we're living no longer fits who we are becoming—each restart is unique, but the ache is familiar. The uncertainty. The disorientation. The quiet fear that maybe, somehow, we've failed.

But what if we reframed the story?

What if beginning again was never a sign of failure—but the natural rhythm of growth, healing, and becoming?

A Story of Starting Over

When I left my home country, I thought it would be temporary. I was a child—small and full of belief that life would return to what it was. I imagined I'd go back to my room, to my friends, to a place where my name didn't need explaining. But instead, I found myself in a refugee camp, sleeping beneath a fabric roof with the sky as my ceiling. My language, my home, my sense of belonging—gone in an instant.

That was my first restart. I did not know it then, but it would not be my last.

Years later, I would move again. Learn new languages. Change schools. Hide my accent. Carry my pain like a secret. I began to equate starting over with erasing myself. With trying harder to blend in. With shrinking the girl I had been before the chaos arrived.

But now, with time and tenderness, I see it differently.

Every restart carried pieces of who I was. Starting over did not mean beginning empty. It meant beginning again—with more wisdom, more depth, more courage. With scars that told stories, and a heart that had seen both the worst and most beautiful parts of the world.

Maybe that's true for you, too.

The Hidden Strength in Beginning Again

Trauma doesn't just affect the mind—it reshapes our sense of identity. It teaches us how to survive, but sometimes at the cost of knowing who we are beneath the surviving.

Maybe you believe you should have held on longer. Spoken up sooner. Maybe you feel behind—like others are ahead while you're still gathering the pieces.

But what if starting over isn't a sign of being behind, but a reflection of deep wisdom?

Each restart—no matter how painful—is an act of resistance. A refusal to settle for what harmed you. A declaration that life still holds something worth reaching for.

Even when you've lost your footing. Even when you've had to let go of people you love. Even when you've released a version of yourself you once believed in—choosing to begin again says, *I still believe in something better.*

And that is not weakness.
That is strength.

Grieving What Didn't Last

Starting over often begins with loss. And loss deserves to be honored.

Sometimes, it's not what happened that breaks us, but what never had the chance to. The childhood we didn't get to live. The dream that never came true. The version of ourselves we never got to become.

Grieving these things is not a failure of perspective—it is a mark of love. Of hope. Of being fully human.

There was a time I tried to skip this part. I told myself to be grateful. I busied my grief into silence. But it caught up with me—in my posture, in my breath, in the way I apologized for simply existing.

Eventually, I sat down and wrote every piece of home I missed. Every version of myself I had left behind to survive. I let myself cry for all that was lost.

And that was the beginning of my healing.

Because when we name what we've lost, we also name what we are worthy of rebuilding.

Anchoring Into What Is Still True

When everything feels uprooted, you need anchors—not the kind that weigh you down, but the kind that remind you who you are.

Your name. Your mother tongue. The lullabies your grandmother sang. The values you hold, even when the world tries to strip them away—these are your roots.

Return to them.

Cook the food that smells like home. Speak your truth in the way your people do. Light a candle. Breathe. Remember your worth.

Create new rituals that hold both your sorrow and your joy.

Your body remembers safety. Your soul remembers peace. Let them lead you back to yourself.

The Soft Power of Reclamation

There is a quiet revolution in choosing to stay soft when the world has tried to harden you.

For a long time, I thought starting over meant I had failed. That I could not hold things together. But now I know that beginning again is sacred. It is the brave work of someone who refuses to settle for anything less than truth.

Every time I choose to begin again, I reclaim the right to be whole. To rest. To be loved—not for how much I achieve, but for simply existing.

That is what I wish for you, too.

Even if no one sees the weight you carry, I see the courage it takes to keep going. To whisper to yourself, *I will try one more time.*

That is not weakness. That is resilience.
And resilience is the language of becoming.

Reflection Questions

- What part of yourself did you leave behind to survive your last season?

- What new truth are you ready to anchor into as you begin again?

- What would a life rooted in your values—not your fear—look like?

- What would it feel like to believe that starting over could be sacred?

You Are Still Becoming

There is no finish line to healing. No single moment when everything suddenly makes sense. But there are hundreds of quiet, holy beginnings.

Mornings when you rise anyway.
Afternoons when you cry and still carry on.
Evenings when you whisper to yourself, *I am still here.*

You are not a failure because something ended.
You are not broken because you've had to rebuild.

You are a masterpiece in motion.
You are still becoming.

And even this restart—this trembling, tender, unpolished beginning—is part of the story that will one day remind someone else:

They can begin again, too.

Tools for the Journey:
Start Again with Intention

You are not starting from scratch. You are starting from the soul.

This beginning is not proof of failure—it is evidence of your courage to try again.

These tools are not meant to rush you forward, but to anchor you deeply.

May they meet you like soft ground beneath your feet. May they remind you: your becoming is still unfolding.

Let the Truth Be Your First Companion

In moments of disorientation, clarity often begins with honesty. Speak three truths aloud—not about what you've achieved, but who you are at your core. Say: *I keep showing up. I love deeply. I believe healing is possible.* These truths are your compass. Even in unfamiliar terrain, you are not lost—you are rooted.

Let the Body Lead When the Mind Is Tired

You do not have to think your way into safety. You can feel your way there. Ground yourself with small practices: plant your feet firmly, take three long breaths, name five things you see. Say your name aloud. Whisper: *I am here now. I am safe.* Let your body believe what your mind is still learning to trust.

Create Safety in Small, Sacred Ways

Safety is not just a place—it is a feeling. A song that feels like home. A scent that brings back peace. A blanket, a book, a quiet voice note. These small acts are not escapes. They are repair. They tell your inner child: *I see you. You are not alone anymore. You are safe with me now.*

Root Forward—Not Backward

Instead of replaying what fell apart, ask: *What do I want to grow toward?* Imagine your life one year from now—not perfect, but peaceful. Who are you with? What feels different? Let your imagination become prayer. Let your future vision pull you gently toward what still matters most.

Reclaim a Piece of What Was Left Behind

Sometimes starting over means bringing something beautiful with you. Is there a ritual, memory, dream, or language you once loved? Return to it. Make your grandmother's recipe. Speak your name in your first tongue. Sing the song you were told to silence. Reclamation is resistance. It says: *I get to decide what I carry forward.*

Speak to Yourself with Soft Authority

You are not behind. You are not broken. You are not foolish for beginning again. Talk to yourself the way you would speak to a beloved child: *"I haven't failed. I'm learning. I am allowed to start over."* Let your voice be the kindest one you hear today. Let it be home.

Release the Rush to Be "Fixed"

Healing does not follow a schedule. There is no finish line for wholeness. You do not have to figure it all out quickly to be worthy of love. Let go of the deadline. Trust the rhythm. What matters most is presence—not performance. Let yourself breathe. Let yourself belong to this moment.

Let Small Moments Mark Your Return

Your healing will not always feel like fireworks. Sometimes, it's the quiet moment when a song soothes your chest. When sunlight touches your skin and you do not flinch. When your own name spoken aloud sounds like love again. These are signs you are returning—not just to life, but to yourself.

Choose Rituals That Welcome You Back

Rituals ground you in rhythm when everything else feels unsteady. Light a candle at dusk. Hum a lullaby you once knew. Write your name slowly and say, *I'm still here.* These are not just gestures. They are reminders: you are worthy of gentleness. You are worthy of beginning again.

Know This Is Sacred Work

Starting over is not a sign of weakness. It is the soft courage of those who have lived through the storm and are still choosing to rise. It is not about erasing what came before. It is about becoming more whole because of it. You are not rebuilding your life from rubble—you are building from wisdom, strength, and soul.

You do not need a roadmap. You need grace.
You do not need to be fearless. You only need to stay faithful—to the next breath, the next choice, the next step.
You are not starting from nothing.
You are starting from everything you have survived.
And that is more than enough.

PART III

Embrace: Hold Your Story with Compassion

You are not broken—you are beautifully surviving.

A tender chapter honoring the quiet strength it takes to carry what no one sees. An invitation to meet yourself with compassion and care.

There comes a time in every healing journey when we no longer need to fight our pain—we need to hold it. And not just the pain, but ourselves. Gently. Tenderly. Like we would hold a friend who has seen too much and still finds the strength to rise.

This part of the journey is about pausing. About laying down the armor we carried for so long—the survival strategies that once kept us safe but now keep us separate. It is about learning, slowly, to offer ourselves what we've always offered others: kindness, compassion, patience.

We are not here to fix what happened. We are here to witness it. To turn inward, to sit beside the girl within us who endured what no one should have to endure, and instead of asking her to be stronger, to simply say: *I see you. I believe you. You've done enough.*

This is where we begin to understand that survival is not a sign of damage—it is a mark of astonishing strength. The fact that we are still here, still breathing, still loving despite it all—that is resilience. That is grace.

In these pages, drawing from teachings inspired by Brené Brown and Dr. Gabor Maté, we will explore what it means to meet shame with tenderness. To wrap even the messiest parts of our story in mercy. When shame says, *You are unworthy,*compassion says, *You've been through so much—and still, you love. Still, you rise.*

This is not a solitary path. Each of us, in quiet ways, carries wounds. But together, we are remembering: pain does not define us—it reveals our courage. And when we honor that courage with gentleness, we begin to come home to ourselves.

So let this be a shared exhale.
Let this be a sacred pause.
Let this be the part of your story where you stop running—and begin resting in your truth.

You are not too broken. You are not too much. And you are not alone. We are walking this road together. And even here—even now—you are worthy of love.

From One Heart to Another —
Feel Deeply, Love Fully   *Letter from a champion*

To the girl who always felt too much and never enough,

You were never the problem.

Not when they told you to shrink to fit in.
Not when they tried to label you—the "quiet Chinese girl," "Black girl," "Indigenous girl," "immigrant girl," the "diversity hire," the "model minority."
Not even when you started believing it.

You learned early on how to read the room. How to make people comfortable.
To work twice as hard, say half as much, and never take up too much space.
And yet, you always carried something bigger inside you—a quiet knowing that the world could be better. Kinder. Fairer.
Even when you didn't have the words for it yet.

There's so much I wish I could tell you.
That the people who love the deepest are often the ones who've been hurt the most—but choose softness anyway.
That the magic you see in others already lives in you.
That being sensitive isn't a flaw. It's a gift.

You'll spend years trying to prove your worth.
You'll succeed in rooms that were never built for you.
And eventually, you'll realize you don't need to fight to belong in them—you were never meant to blend in.

You were meant to stand out.
To speak up.
To spark change.
And oh, how you will.

You'll build a career and a life rooted in values, not validation.
You'll create a podcast to amplify stories that deserve to be heard—not because it's your job, but because it's your calling.
You'll raise daughters who speak boldly and love wildly—and they'll remind you that healing is possible in this lifetime.
You'll stand on stages and finally feel the truth: You were never too much. You were just ahead of your time.

To every girl who has been underestimated, misunderstood, or made to feel small—
I see you. I am you.

You are love. You are light. You are allowed to be loud, soft, fierce, messy, joyful—and still a work in progress.
You don't need to go looking for magic. You are it.
And the world needs more of what only you can give.

Keep going.

With all my heart,
Jenny Chen

CHAPTER 7

To the Girl Who Carries Quiet Grief —

Your sadness is sacred. Let it breathe.

My love,

I see the way you carry it—in your silence, in your eyes, in the way you smile gently so others feel comfortable, even when your own heart feels heavy. Not everyone notices, but I do. I see how you hold it all together while quietly falling apart.

There is a kind of grief that doesn't make itself loud. It doesn't come with flowers or funerals or permission to fall apart. It lives quietly inside you—steady, unseen. It shows up in stillness, when the world stops moving and no one is watching. It hides in the way you pause before answering. In the way you carry your body like it remembers loss too well.

This grief may not have a name that others understand. Maybe it's for someone you lost. Or a place that once felt like home. Maybe it's for a childhood cut short. A version of yourself you never got to become. A dream you had to let go of before you were ready.

Whatever it is, please Know: Your grief is not a weakness. It is a form of love with nowhere to go. And that makes it part of your becoming.

You do not need permission to feel it. You do not owe anyone an explanation for why it still hurts. Grief doesn't follow a timeline. There is no "too long" when it comes to mourning what mattered.

So let yourself feel what you feel. Cry when you need to. Rest when it's heavy. Speak their name if you want to. Write the words you never got to say. Light the candle. Take the walk. Sing the song. Let your sadness breathe.

You were never meant to carry it alone.

There is space for your sorrow here. And in time, there will be space for joy again, too.

But for now, just remember this:
Your sadness is not something to hide.
It is proof that you loved. That you hoped. That you tried.

And that, my dear, is something beautiful.

With all my heart,
Someone who sees your quiet strength

Life Lesson:
Let Grief Breathe

Some grief is loud. It wails and floods and makes its presence known. But there is another kind of grief—quieter, slower, often invisible to the world. It lives in small, sacred places: behind brave smiles, in the silence between words, in the hush of late-night stillness when no one else can see.

This is the grief many of us carry quietly. And this chapter is for that kind.

I was only a child the first time I felt it—that hollow ache in the chest when something precious is gone and there are no words big enough to name the loss. I remember walking through school hallways after we fled our home. I looked like any other student, but inside, I was grieving a thousand invisible things: my room, my friends, my sense of safety, the innocence of a childhood I would never fully return to.

Grief moved in like an uninvited guest who never left. But because there were no ceremonies for the kind of losses I endured, I didn't know how to mourn. So I tucked it away. I tried to be strong. I stayed busy. I smiled a lot.

Years later, I found myself doing the same after the death of my daughter. That grief was louder, but just as isolating. People do not always know how to sit with deep sorrow. They want you to be okay. They want the version of you they once knew. And when you are not, it can feel like you are letting the world down.

But grief changes you. It shifts the shape of your soul. It teaches you about the fragility of life and the depth of love. It humbles you. It softens you. It breaks you open.

And what I have learned is That: grief never truly leaves. It evolves. Some days, it whispers. Other days, it returns as a wave. Both are valid. Both are sacred.

The goal isn't to "get over it." The goal is to make space for it—to allow your heart to carry grief with tenderness, not fear.

Learning to Sit With the Ache

There is no timeline for grief. No finish line. No single way it should look. You do not need to cry to prove it hurts. You do not need to stay silent to appear strong.

Sometimes, healing looks like telling their story again. Saying their name out loud. Lighting a candle in their honor. Dancing to a song you once shared. Writing a letter you will never send.

Sometimes, healing is just making it through the day.

You are not weak for missing someone years later. You are not broken for still aching. You are human.

We live in a world that rushes healing. That wants quick fixes and tidy endings. But soul-level healing asks for something else: honesty, presence, and permission to feel what is real.

That kind of presence is not weakness. It is courage—the kind that opens the door to real healing.

Compassion as a Way Forward

There is a unique kind of love that grief teaches us—raw, unfiltered, and full of grace. Once you have felt deep sorrow, you begin to understand the sacredness of tenderness.

So begin with yourself.

Talk to yourself the way you would speak to someone you love. When you wake up with a heavy heart, whisper: *It's okay. I'm still here. You are not alone.* When the tears come, let them. When your heart feels full again, welcome the joy, too.

Grief and joy can live side by side. You do not have to choose one over the other.

Some of the kindest, most radiant souls I know carry deep sorrow. Their hearts are wide because they have learned to hold both ache and awe. Their love runs deep because they have made peace with absence.

When you let your grief breathe, you create space for compassion— not only for yourself, but for others. You begin to recognize the pain behind someone else's eyes. You speak more gently. You become a safe place. You live more fully.

Tending to the Child Within

For those of us who carried grief as children, part of the work is going back for the girl who was never allowed to mourn. The one who was told to be strong. To move on. To act as though the loss never happened.

She still lives within you. And she is waiting.

Sometimes I close my eyes and sit beside her. I say, *I'm so sorry you had to carry that alone. You didn't deserve that pain. You matter to me.*

We all deserve to hear those words. And when we say them to our inner child, we begin to restore the parts of ourselves that learned to grieve in silence.

Your Sadness Is Sacred

Not everyone will understand. Some will try to fix you. Others may ask you to hurry your healing. That does not mean your grief is wrong. It simply means they have not yet learned how to honor sorrow.

But you can.

You can treat your grief as sacred.
You can let it shape you with softness instead of shame.
You can allow it to teach you about love—not as something lost, but as something still alive within you.

You do not have to be okay to be loved.
You do not have to be cheerful to belong.
You do not have to be healed to be worthy.

You are already all of those things.

This Is What Strength Looks Like

Strength is not pretending you are fine.
It is not silencing your pain.
Strength is letting your story breathe.

It is choosing not to numb.
It is choosing to feel.
It is learning to hold your sadness with care.

You are not broken because you grieve.
You are beautifully surviving.

So let this be your permission:
To stop running from the ache.
To sit with it.
To honor it.
To let it show you how deeply you can love.

You are not alone.
Your sadness is sacred. Let it breathe.

And in time—you will too.

Tools for the Journey:
Honour the Quiet Grief You Carry

Grief that hides beneath your smile deserves as much tenderness as pain the world can see.

When you carry sorrow the world cannot name, it can feel like living in a quiet room while everyone else rushes past in noise.

Invisible sorrow is its own kind of loneliness. It does not come with ceremonies or casseroles. It rarely earns days off or tender understanding. And yet—it shapes the way you breathe, the way you trust, the way you hope.

These tools are not about "moving on."
They are about moving with—your sadness, your story, your full humanity.
They are not prescriptions. They are invitations.
Not for performance, but for presence.
Not to fix what happened, but to help you hold it with gentleness and grace.

Let them be your quiet companions.
Let them remind you:
You are not broken because you still hurt.
You are truth because you are still here.

Name the Ache, Even If No One Else Can See It

Invisible grief still bruises. Even when no one else acknowledges it, your soul remembers. Speak your sorrow—not for validation, but for reverence. Whisper it to your reflection. Write it in a letter. Let it take shape. Naming your grief does not make it heavier—it makes it sacred.

Let Your Body Speak the Language of Loss

When words cannot carry the weight, your body tries. The tight jaw. The aching shoulders. The exhaustion that makes no sense. Trust its messages. Walk slowly. Stretch gently. Cry without apology. Rock yourself if that feels kind. Movement is not weakness—it is release.

Create Rituals That Remember What Was Real

When there is no funeral for what you lost, make your own small ceremony. Light a candle at dawn. Drink tea in silence. Hold an object that carries memory. Ritual is how you honor what mattered. It says to your soul: *This happened. And I still care.*

Speak to Yourself with Fierce Mercy

Grief is already heavy—do not let shame add weight. When the inner critic says *"It wasn't that bad"* or *"You should be over it,"* answer with truth: *"This matters. I matter. I am healing in my own time."* Compassion is not weakness—it is an act of survival.

Find Places Where Grief Doesn't Need a Mask

It is exhausting to pretend. You need spaces where your sorrow can stretch without being questioned. This may be a forest trail, a quiet corner of your room, or a friend who says, *"You don't have to explain."* Seek what feels safe. Let it be your sanctuary.

Let Beauty Coexist with Your Grief

Joy is not betrayal. It is breath. Even in sorrow, beauty finds a way in—a breeze, a song, the way the sky shifts color at dusk. Let yourself notice it. Let it soften the edges. These glimmers are not distraction. They are reminders: *I am still alive. I can still feel.*

Feel It Fully—Without Trying to Fix It

There is no map for grief. Some days you will ache without knowing why. Some days you will laugh through tears. It's all valid. Healing is not about controlling the waves—it's about learning to float. Let it be messy. Let it be yours.

Write to the People You Miss—
Even If They're Not Listening

Letters are bridges. Even if no one reads them, they free what's been trapped inside. Write to those you lost. Or to the version of yourself you miss. Say what was never said. These words are not about response. They are about release.

Allow the Grief to Move—But Not Take Over

You are not your sadness. It moves through you like rain through soil. Let it pass without becoming it. Say to yourself, *"This pain is real, but it is not the whole of me."* Grief may shape you, but it does not define you. You still belong to joy, too.

Come Home to the Breath That Stayed

When everything else feels like it's falling away, your breath remains. Place a hand on your chest. Inhale for four counts. Hold. Exhale slowly. This is proof: *You are still here. You are still becoming. You are still worthy of peace.*

A Quiet Kind of Courage

You do not need loud strength to survive grief. You need softness. Slowness. Truth. Grief is not a flaw. It is a testimony to how deeply you loved, how deeply you lived. So let your sadness breathe. Let your tenderness speak. Let your story unfold with no need to rush. And above all, let yourself be held—by the quiet, by the breath, by your own sacred becoming.

CHAPTER 8

To the Girl Learning to Forgive Herself —

You are worthy of your own gentleness.

There are moments that replay in your mind—not because you want them to, but because some part of you believes you should have known better. Done better. Been better.

If that's where you find yourself today, I want to sit beside you—not with answers or advice, but with softness.

Forgiveness is not forgetting. It is not pretending the pain never happened, or brushing past the choices you wish you had not made. It is not excusing harm or rewriting the truth.

Forgiveness—especially the kind we offer ourselves—is a sacred act of love. It is a quiet but powerful declaration: *Even in my most imperfect hour, I was still worthy of compassion.* I was trying. I was learning. I was surviving.

Maybe you carry guilt rooted in trauma. Maybe you blame yourself for not being able to stop something that was never your fault. Maybe you silenced parts of who you were just to make it through—and now you're grieving the girl you used to be.

That grief is real. And so is the healing that follows.

This letter is not a push. It is a permission slip. To take your time. To listen gently to the part of you that is tired of carrying shame. To whisper back to your heart, *I hear you. I see how hard you've tried. I'm not here to punish you—I'm here to love you back to life.*

Forgiveness does not begin with resolution. It begins with presence. With sitting still. With returning to yourself, breath by breath. With holding the hand of the girl you were when everything fell apart—and saying to her, *You didn't deserve the weight you carried. You did the best you could with what you knew. And that matters.*

There is no deadline for healing. No rulebook for how long it should take. There is only this moment. And in this moment, you are already enough.

You are not your mistakes.
You are not your silence.
You are not your shame.

You are someone who is learning how to love herself again.
And I promise you—there is nothing more powerful than that.

With tenderness,
The one who knows you are worthy of your own gentleness

Life Lesson:
You Are Worthy of Your Own Gentleness

There are few things heavier than the weight we carry when we believe we should have known better, done better, or been better. For many of us, forgiveness is not a destination—it is a slow and sacred path back to our own hearts. Especially when the one we struggle to forgive is ourselves.

Let us begin not with the wisdom of resolution, but with the honesty of wounds.

Because most of us are not taught how to forgive ourselves. We are taught how to critique ourselves. How to shrink to fit expectations. How to measure our worth by achievements. How to internalize the disappointment in someone else's eyes. We learn shame before we learn softness. Survival before self-love.

But survival, beautiful girl, is not the same as self-compassion.

Let Me Tell You a Story

There was a time when I was navigating life in a new country, carrying invisible grief in a place that didn't recognize my past. I made choices that felt like survival. I stayed silent when I wanted to speak. I performed happiness while my heart was breaking. I betrayed parts of myself just to feel safe enough to belong.

Years later, I looked back on that version of myself—not with compassion, but with blame. *How could I? Why didn't I know better?*

And so I punished myself quietly—through perfectionism, overworking, and striving endlessly for redemption I didn't think I deserved.

But here is what I had to learn, softly and slowly:
I was doing the best I could with what I had.

And so were you.

You may carry shame for not protecting yourself sooner. For staying too long. For leaving too early. For abandoning your truth in exchange for safety.

But hear this clearly: your silence was not a flaw. Your choices made sense in the context of your fear, your hope, and your humanity.

Forgiveness is not about pretending it didn't hurt.
It is about acknowledging the pain—and choosing, at last, to stop punishing yourself for it.

It is looking back at the girl you once were and saying, *I see you. You were trying. And I love you for that.*

Naming the Shame

Shame thrives in silence. It says not just that you did something wrong—but that *you are* something wrong. It isolates. It whispers that if people really knew you, they would walk away—and that maybe, if you were honest with yourself, you would too.

But what if the opposite is true?

What if bringing your shame into the light is what sets you free? What if your story—exactly as it is—isn't a disqualification but an invitation? To deeper love. To deeper healing. To deeper wholeness.

I once told a mentor, "I don't know how to forgive myself."

She paused and said, *"Start by listening to the voice inside you that has been waiting to be held—not fixed."*

So I began to write letters to myself. Not perfect ones—real ones.

I wrote, *"I miss who I was before I began shrinking."*
Then later, *"I'm ashamed of how I coped."*
And finally, *"I understand now. You did what you needed to do to survive."*

Forgiveness begins with listening.
And listening requires stillness.

The Fear of Letting Go

We sometimes resist self-forgiveness because we confuse it with letting ourselves off the hook. But there is a difference between accountability and shame.

Accountability says, *What did I learn, and how do I want to show up now?*
Shame says, *I am the mistake.*

And when we believe we are the mistake, we live small. We reject joy. We close our hearts. We think we deserve less.

But if you can separate your worth from your wounds, you can rebuild. Not from perfection—but from presence.
Not because you have something to prove, but because you have something to reclaim.

You are not a mistake. You are a human being who is learning.

The Power of Witnessing Yourself

Sometimes the most radical act of healing is simply to witness yourself without judgment. To revisit the memories you regret and softly say, *I see you.* Not to change the story—but to sit with it. To feel its weight. To say, *And even here, I am still worthy.*

Maybe you journal. Maybe you cry at the kitchen sink. Maybe you walk through the woods and let the trees hold your confessions. Whatever it looks like—let yourself be seen, even if only by you.

When you become a safe place for yourself, the world begins to feel less threatening.

Reclaiming Joy

Self-forgiveness opens the door to joy. Not because everything is resolved—but because you are no longer hiding from yourself.

Joy is not a reward for being perfect.
It is your birthright.

You may wake up one day and realize you're not bracing against yourself anymore. That the inner critic has grown quiet, and the inner nurturer has grown strong. You will look at the girl you once were and say, *Thank you. You held on long enough to get me here.*

You Deserve Your Own Mercy

You do not need to earn your way back to your own love.
You already belong to yourself.

Every time you speak gently to the parts of you that still hurt, you are healing.
Every time you whisper, *"I forgive you,"* even if your voice trembles, you are healing.
Every time you say, *"I am still learning, and that is okay,"* you are healing.

Forgiveness is not linear. It loops. It returns. But each time you practice it, your capacity for love—especially for yourself—deepens.

Let this be the beginning.
Not of pretending everything is okay, but of knowing *you* are okay, even when everything is not.

Let this be the day you turn toward yourself with mercy.

You are not broken.
You are beautifully surviving.

And you, brave one, are already enough.

Tools for the Journey:
Forgive Yourself with Grace

Forgiveness is often taught as something we extend to others. But the deepest kind is the kind we give ourselves. Quietly. Repeatedly. Without fanfare.

This is not about pretending it didn't happen. It's about deciding that your past no longer gets to define your becoming.

These tools are not about fixing you—because you are not broken. They are tender invitations. Gentle companions for the holy, human work of coming home to yourself.

Begin with Curiosity, Not Condemnation

When regret knocks, soften your voice. Instead of "What's wrong with me?" ask, "What was I trying to survive?" Most of our choices, even the ones we ache over, were attempts to feel safe, seen, or loved. Forgiveness begins with understanding, not shame.

Speak to Yourself Like You Would a Child

You would not shame a child into healing. You would hold her close and whisper, "You didn't know. But I love you anyway." That voice—the one filled with mercy—is the one you are allowed to use on yourself now.

Rewrite the Scripts You Inherited

You may still carry beliefs that do not belong to you:

"I have to earn love."
"Mistakes make me unworthy."

Pause. Ask: Whose voice is that? And does it still serve me?

Now write a new one: "I am allowed to be human and still be loved."

Welcome Back the Parts of You You've Tried to Exile

Forgiveness is not erasure. It is integration. It is saying to your younger self, "You were doing your best with what you knew. And I am not leaving you behind." You don't need to abandon who you were—you only need to embrace her.

Create Gentle Rituals of Release

Healing needs shape. Write a letter from your future self to the one still holding shame. Light a candle. Whisper, "I release you." These rituals are not dramatic—they are sacred thresholds into softer beginnings.

Let "I am Still Learning" Be Enough

You are not a finished product. You are a living, breathing work-in-progress. Let go of the myth of perfection. Try saying, "I am learning," when shame tries to shout. Let grace be your new language.

Let Others Mirror What You Struggle to See

When you cannot see your own goodness, borrow the eyes of those who love you. Let their words reflect the truth until it becomes your own. Not because they need to convince you—but because you were never meant to heal alone.

Be Tender With the Setbacks

Sometimes, pain returns just when you thought you had moved on. That is not failure—it is the spiral of healing. Let each return be softer. Let it teach you that healing is not a line—it is a rhythm. And your rhythm is still holy.

Release the Lie of "Deserving"

You do not have to earn your own love. You do not have to prove you are worthy of gentleness. You belong to grace. Even in your regret. Even in your learning. Even now.

Make Self-Tenderness a Daily Ritual

Forgiveness is not a one-time vow. It is how you nourish yourself. How you speak to yourself. How you choose rest over punishment. Each time you choose softness, you whisper:

I am still here.
I am still becoming.
I am still worthy of love.

Come Home to Yourself—Again and Again

You are not too far gone. You are not your past. You are a living story still unfolding.

Let this be the moment you stop waiting to be "better" and start believing you are already enough.

Come back to your breath.
Back to mercy.
Back to yourself.

Not someday.
But now.

CHAPTER 9

To the Girl Who Feels Unseen and Still Keeps Going —

Your strength is not invisible. It is radiant—even in silence.

Even when the world does not see you.
Even when the room overlooks you.
Even when the applause lands elsewhere, and no one seems to notice the quiet weight you've been carrying for so long.

Still, you keep going.

You show up. You care. You carry. You tend to others with patience and grace, holding everything together without asking for praise. You move through your days like it's normal to hold so much—and maybe, by now, it is.

But hear me: just because no one says *thank you,* just because no one pauses to ask how *you're* doing, does **not** mean you are any less worthy of being seen, held, or celebrated.

Sometimes the strongest souls are the ones who were never taught how to ask for help—because they were always the helper.

Sometimes the most powerful kind of strength is the kind that whispers instead of shouts.

The kind that wakes up again and again, even when it feels like no one is watching.

The kind that stays soft, even when the world has been hard.

If this is you—if you are the one who holds space for others while your own heart aches—know this:

Your strength is not invisible.

It is radiant.
It is real.
It is worthy of being witnessed.

It lives in the way you keep loving, even when you feel unloved.
It lives in your quiet perseverance.
It lives in your refusal to give up on the people you care for, even when no one sees how much it costs you.

You are not weak for longing to be noticed.
You are not selfish for wanting someone to ask, *"How are you really?"*
That longing to be seen is not something to be ashamed of—it is profoundly human.

And while the world may take time to catch up to your light, I hope you will not wait to see yourself.

I hope you pause.
I hope you whisper your name with tenderness.
I hope you look in the mirror and remember that just being here is an act of quiet brilliance.

You do not have to perform your worth to earn it.
You do not need applause to be worthy of love.
You are already enough.
Already radiant.
Already whole.

You deserve to be seen.
You deserve to be cared for—not only when you fall apart, but also when you're holding it all together.

So this is for you, love—
The one who feels unseen and keeps going anyway.

I see you now.
And you are everything.

With all my heart,
Someone who sees you now.

Life Lesson:
The Strength No One Sees

There is a certain kind of strength that rarely gets acknowledged. It does not shout. It does not perform. It does not arrive with applause or spotlight. Instead, it lingers quietly in the corners of ordinary days—in the way you show up, even when no one sees you. In the way you love, even when you feel forgotten. In the way you keep going, even when your name is never called.

Today, I want to speak to that kind of strength.
I want to speak to you.

Because I know what it means to walk into rooms and feel invisible.
To do everything "right," and still be overlooked.
To hold your sadness with grace.
To carry others when you are tired yourself.
To wonder—*does any of it matter?*

There are so many of us living with that ache.
And still, we rise.
Still, we give.
Still, we carry on.

When Strength Becomes a Disguise

When I was a teenager in a new country, I became very quiet—not because I had nothing to say, but because my voice felt foreign, unfamiliar, out of place. I was praised for how "well I adapted," but no one saw the energy it took to smile, to participate, to keep my mask from slipping. I got good at being agreeable. I followed the rules. I helped where I could. But inside, I was aching to be known for more than what I could offer.

So many young women learn early that their value lies in their usefulness—in how much space they do not take up. We're taught that strength means self-sacrifice. That to be loved, we must be easy, pleasant, productive.

Over time, we begin to believe that the only way to belong is to become smaller.

We become the helper, the peacemaker, the dependable one— until our identity disappears into other people's needs.

And when no one sees the effort, the effort begins to feel invisible too.

Eventually, we begin to feel invisible.

You Are Not Invisible

But let me tell you this truth: you are not invisible.

Your presence matters, even when it is not recognized.
Your strength is not erased just because it is quiet.
Your radiance may not demand attention—but it changes the atmosphere.
Your love may not be loud—but it lingers.

Your consistency. Your compassion. Your courage to keep going— these are sacred.
And the first person who needs to see them… is you.

When Silence Is Mistaken for Strength

I used to believe that strength meant silence. That if I stayed composed, if I held everything in, someone would notice and offer what I needed. I thought that if I never asked for anything, I would finally receive what I longed for.

But what I didn't understand was this:

Silence is not always strength.
Sometimes, it is fear.
Sometimes, it is a habit we learned because no one listened when
we first tried to speak.

If you were the strong one in your family, your friend group, your
community—you know this well. You were praised for being steady,
responsible, mature. But did anyone ask what it cost you?

Did anyone tell you that you deserve to be held too?

The Myth of the Invisible Girl

There is a myth many of us carry:
If I am good, I will be loved.
If I am helpful, I will be wanted.
If I do not cause trouble, someone will stay.

And so we mold ourselves into what others need, hoping someone
will finally see us.

But wholeness doesn't come from disappearing.
It comes from being known.

To the girl who feels unseen:
You do not need to be louder to matter.
But you do deserve to be heard.

And it starts by listening inward—to the part of you that is tired
of pretending, tired of performing, tired of pouring from an
empty cup.

Your Light Is Real

There is a kind of light that lives in you.
It may not shine in the ways the world expects.
It may not get you trophies or titles.
But it is no less powerful.

It is the light that notices others when no one else does.
The light that holds space without needing recognition.
The light that survives because it has always had to.

That light is sacred.
And it deserves to be honored—not only by others, but by you.

When the Applause Doesn't Come

One of the loneliest things is doing the right thing—the hard thing—when no one is watching.

Telling the truth.
Choosing kindness.
Walking away from what harms you.
Holding boundaries.
Starting over.

These acts require immense courage.
But they do not always come with affirmation.

Still, I want you to know: your healing is not a performance.
It does not require a stage.
It is allowed to be private.
It is allowed to be quiet.
It is allowed to be for you.

And even when no one claps—what you are doing is powerful.

You Were Never Meant to Carry It All Alone

Perhaps the most dangerous belief we inherit is that being strong means being alone.
That asking for help is weakness.
That needing support disqualifies us from being brave.

But the truth is: we were never meant to do this by ourselves.
We were meant to be held. To be seen. To be met with care.

If you haven't found those spaces yet, do not give up.

Keep searching for the people who speak gently to your soul.
Keep building spaces where your presence is honored.

And while you search, begin by becoming that space for yourself.

Speak to yourself the way you've longed to be spoken to.
Wrap your arms around the girl who tried so hard to be good enough—and tell her:

You don't have to earn your place here.
You belong.
You are already enough.

Let This Be Your Quiet Revolution

To the girl who keeps going, even when no one claps:

Your strength is not invisible.
It is written into your breath.
It lives in your tenderness.
It shows up in your quiet refusal to give up.

The world may not always reflect your worth back to you.
But that does not mean it is not there.

You are not invisible. You are luminous.

Let this be your quiet revolution:
Not to shout louder, but to live deeper.
Not to fight for a seat at the table, but to build one where your voice is cherished.
Where your heart is safe.
Where your strength is not just noticed—but nurtured.

And may you always remember:
You do not have to be seen by everyone to be seen by yourself.
And that is where your light begins to shine.

Tools for the Journey:
Honour the Power That Moves Quietly

Some forms of strength are loud. Public. Celebrated. But not all courage looks like a battle cry. This is for the girl who feels unseen and still keeps going—Not because you need to be fixed or found, but because strength that lives in silence deserves to be recognized, nurtured, and held with tenderness.

We live in a world that celebrates the loudest voices, the boldest wins, the most visible achievements. But some of the deepest resilience blooms in quiet. In the way you rise and tend to life when your name is not called. In the way you hold space for others while silently longing to be held yourself.

This is the journey of reclaiming your quiet strength. Of choosing to see yourself, even when the world does not. Of remembering that your worth is not dependent on applause—but rooted in your humanity.

Learn to Witness Your Own Strength

There is a shift that happens when you stop waiting to be seen and start learning how to see yourself. It does not mean you stop longing for connection—it means you stop measuring your worth by someone else's gaze. Start by noticing your strength in the smallest, bravest acts: the mornings you rose despite heaviness, the moments you stayed soft when life invited you to harden. Let those moments count. Let them define you.

Create a Ritual of Recognition

Set aside five quiet minutes each day. Name one act of quiet strength. Maybe you comforted someone while your own spirit ached. Maybe you rested instead of performing. Maybe you made yourself tea and didn't rush. These are not small. These are sacred. Write them down. Speak them aloud. Let them become the evidence of your becoming.

Name What Was Missing Without Shame

If no one ever celebrated your small victories, it is okay to say so. If no one noticed how much you carried, or how much you gave—it is okay to grieve that. This is not self-pity. It is soul truth. It is how we begin to re-parent the heart that went unnoticed. Say it. Mourn it. Then offer yourself the love you were denied.

Let Rest Be a Sacred Declaration

When you grow up feeling unseen, rest can feel like laziness. Joy can feel unearned. But you are allowed to exhale. To laugh. To soften into stillness. Rest is not a reward. Joy is not a privilege. They are your right. Let them be your quiet rebellion. Let them remind your body: I matter, even when I am not producing.

Redefine What Strength Means to You

Strength is not endurance at all costs. It is not silent suffering. It is the ability to feel—to weep, to need, to ask. Maybe your new definition of strong sounds like: "I cannot do this alone." Or "I deserve to be loved without performing." Or "I am worthy of softness, too." Let that be enough. Let that be everything.

Surround Yourself with Soul-Affirming People

You do not need to earn love by being useful. You do not need to dim to stay connected. Seek the people who make space for your whole self—your questions, your softness, your radiance. Sometimes they come later in life. Sometimes you become that person for yourself first. But never stop believing they exist. They do.

A Final Whisper to Carry With You

You are not invisible. You are luminous.
Even in your silence.
Even in your weariness.
Even when no one claps or calls your name.

You were never meant to live in the shadows.
You were meant to rise—quietly, slowly, honestly—
until your life reflects the truth that has always been yours:
You are not here to be overlooked.
You are here to belong.

And you do.

From One Heart to Another —
Let Your Light Lead

Letter from a champion

Dear Girl Holding Back Her Light,

I am writing to you with so much tenderness—
because I remember you.

The girl who used to laugh a little louder, dream a little wilder, and speak a little more freely. I remember how, somewhere between the ages of 8 and 10, the world began whispering rules into your ear. Not all at once. But slowly. Quietly. Enough to make you second-guess that voice inside you.

You were told to be polite.
To be good.
To be sweet.
To not take up too much space.
To not talk back.
To not draw too much attention.
To not be too proud—even when you worked so hard for something.
To shrink just enough to make others feel comfortable.

And maybe, like so many of us, you listened. Not because you wanted to disappear. But because you thought being loved meant being less.

And over time, that light of yours? It started to dim.

Not because it was not bright enough—but because the world convinced you it was too bright.

By the time we become women, we have spent years putting everyone else's needs ahead of our own. We know how to be kind, humble, supportive, and silent. But somewhere along the way, we forget how to belong to ourselves.

So today, I want to remind you:
You are allowed to belong to yourself.

To your thoughts. Your dreams. Your joy. Your voice.
You are allowed to be led by your own inner compass—the one that always knows what feels true, what feels aligned, what brings peace. That voice is still there. It always has been.

Hold on to her.

And if you feel like you've lost her—go looking. Sit quietly. Ask yourself what matters. What lights you up. What hurts. What heals. Then start honoring the answers that rise within you.

Because a happy life—a deeply fulfilling life—cannot be built from the outside in. It must come from within. From what you know to be true. Even if others don't yet understand it.

Now, let me tell you a secret about resilience.

Resilience isn't about never falling.
It is about learning how to rise—again and again—without letting the world harden your heart or silence your dreams.

Resilience is choosing to believe in what's possible,
even after disappointment.
It is letting your story grow roots and wings, not shame.
It is whispering to yourself, "I'm not done yet," even when the world tells you to quit.

Our dear friend Solange—who is writing this beautiful book you hold in your hands—is one of the many examples of that kind of resilience.

I have watched her rise more times than I can count. I have watched her pursue her dreams in a world that did not always understand her. And she did it not just for herself, but for others—for girls like you, and women like me. She did it with heart, with grace, and in service of something greater than herself.

And she is not alone. I could tell you stories of countless women like her—warriors in silence, mothers of dreams, architects of hope—who kept going even when it was hard. Women who remembered who they were and chose to live as if they mattered. Because they do. And so do you.

So as you read this letter,
May you always find the light within you.
May you always come back to your voice, even if it trembles.
May you be rooted in truth, led by purpose, and held by grace.
And when life asks you to rise, may you do so again and again—braver each time.

With love, belief, and sisterhood,
Zel

PART IV

Awaken: Shine the Light Within

You were never too much. You have always been enough.

A call to reclaim your worth, reconnect with your dreams, and rise into the light that has always lived inside you.

You were never too much. You have always been enough.

There comes a moment in every healing journey where the quiet turns into clarity.
Where the tenderness we've offered ourselves begins to illuminate the path ahead.
This is that moment.

After walking through grief, facing what hurt us, and learning to hold our stories with compassion, we arrive here—not because the pain has vanished, but because we have grown brave enough to meet ourselves in its presence.
And now, we are ready to rise.

This part of our journey is not about becoming someone new.
It is about *remembering* who we were before the world told us to shrink.
Before shame taught us to dim.
Before fear whispered that we were too much.

It is about reclaiming our inner radiance—the part of us that has always been quietly burning, even beneath the weight of doubt or the shadow of silence.
The part of us that never stopped glowing, even in the dark.

We are awakening—not into perfection, but into presence.
Into purpose.
Into truth.

We are awakening into the knowing that our voice matters.
That our dreams are not accidents.
That our fullness is not something to hide, but something to honour.
That the light we carry is not a mistake—it is a guide.

This is where we begin to move differently in the world.
Not just surviving. Not just coping.
But allowing ourselves to *expand*.

We give ourselves permission to:

- Take up space.
- Follow joy.
- Speak truths aloud that we once only whispered.
- Walk away from what no longer fits.
- Step into rooms like we belong—because we do.

We stop apologizing for our brilliance.
We stop asking for permission to be seen.
We stop waiting for the world to tell us we are worthy—because we already know.

Together, let us rise—
Not with grand declarations or performance,
But with the grounded grace of those who know what it costs to stay dim,
And who are no longer willing to pay that price.

Let this be our gentle awakening.
Let this be the beginning of the life we were always meant to live.
Let this be the chapter where we remember:

We were never too much.
We have always been enough.
And now—**it is time to shine.**

CHAPTER 10

To the Girl Who Was Told She's "Too Much"—

You are here to overflow.

There is a particular ache that comes from being called "too much."

Too loud.
Too emotional.
Too intense.
Too sensitive.
Too ambitious.
Too different.

It can make you question whether your presence is a burden. Whether your joy is too bright. Whether your voice takes up too much space. Whether your dreams are inconvenient. Whether your light makes others squint.

If you have ever tried to make yourself smaller so others could breathe easier—this letter is for you.

My love, you were never too much. You were simply standing in a world that had forgotten how to hold the fullness of a woman becoming.

You were never the problem. You were the mirror.

A mirror that reflected truth in a world that preferred silence. A mirror that radiated possibility in spaces that had settled for playing it safe. A mirror that dared to dream louder than what others had the courage to imagine.

And yes, sometimes that made them uncomfortable. But their discomfort was never your responsibility.

You were made to feel deeply. To speak boldly. To live fully. To overflow—with energy, with vision, with fire, with love.

That is not *too much.*
That is power.

You do not need to edit your essence to be worthy of belonging. The right people, the right spaces, the right dreams will not require you to shrink. They will rise to meet your light.

There will always be those who do not understand your depth. Who feel threatened by your joy. Who mistake your passion for chaos. Who want you quiet, contained, predictable. Let them go.

You are not here to be digestible. You are here to be real.
To be magic.
To be whole.

You were never too much. You were always more than enough. And you still are.

So take up your space. Speak your truth. Let your laugh echo. Let your tears fall freely. Let your ideas be big. Let your love be bigger.

Overflow, love.

Because the world needs what only your "too much" can give.

With you in all your wild, radiant glory,
—**Solange**

Even when they tried to shrink you. Even when your laughter was labeled disruptive, your ideas dismissed, your emotions deemed excessive. Even when you were told to tone it down, soften your voice, dim your fire—you kept glowing.

And maybe, somewhere along the way, you started to wonder: *Is it really too much? Am I?*

This is what happens when the world isn't ready for a girl who dares to show up fully. It tries to make her doubt herself. It praises the quiet, rewards the agreeable, and celebrates the small. But you, love, were not born for containment. You were born to be expansive.

Your dreams are not outrageous. Your passion is not overwhelming. Your feelings are not inconvenient. They are the pulse of your aliveness—the living, breathing proof that you are awake in a world that often numbs itself.

You were never meant to shrink just to make others more comfortable. You were meant to stir something in people. To light up rooms. To ask the harder questions. To feel what others are too afraid to feel.

Maybe they called you dramatic because they didn't know how to hold your sadness.
Maybe they called you loud because your truth threatened their silence.
Maybe they called you intense because your light cast shadows they weren't ready to face.

But hear this: the fire in you was never meant to be extinguished. It was meant to warm. To illuminate. To blaze trails others never thought to walk.

You are not too much. You are whole. You are sacred.
You are a force.

And no—you do not need to dial yourself down to be loved. The right people will never ask you to.

Your voice belongs. Your tears belong. Your joy, your anger, your softness, your depth, your complexity—*they all belong.*

So take up space. Reclaim your fullness. Let your presence be the love letter you never received. Let your story be the permission someone else is still waiting for.

Overflow, love. Not out of defiance, but out of truth. Not to prove your worth, but because you remember it now.

You were never too much.
You were always the beginning of something more.

With you in your fullness,
Someone who sees you clearly now

Life Lesson:
Embrace the Fullness of Who You Are

There is something undeniably radiant about a girl who feels deeply, speaks boldly, laughs loudly, and dreams without shrinking. And yet, for so many of us, that very radiance has been labeled "too much." Too loud. Too emotional. Too passionate. Too opinionated. Too sensitive. Too ambitious. Too wild. Too big.

Too much—for who?

I remember the first time someone told me I was "too much." I had answered a question in school with too much enthusiasm. I spoke with fire in my voice, and I remember the way the classroom fell silent afterward—not in awe, but in discomfort. A classmate said gently but firmly, "Tone it down; you're too intense." I carried that moment like a hidden scar. It wasn't just about the volume of my voice—it was about what my spirit represented. From that day forward, I tried to edit myself. I made my laugh quieter. My dreams smaller. My presence less visible. I was afraid of eclipsing others. Afraid of rejection. Afraid of standing too brightly in my own light.

And maybe you know this feeling too—the internal tug-of-war between being true to yourself and trying to be palatable. The desire to be fully expressed clashing with the fear of being labeled, mocked, or abandoned. The exhaustion of performing a diluted version of your truth.

But here's what I've come to learn—what I want you to hear deeply and clearly: You are not too much. You are whole. And the world has always needed the fullness of who you are.

The Lie of "Too Much"

What people call "too much" is often what they don't understand—or what threatens what they've grown used to. A girl who weeps at injustice, who challenges power, who refuses to stay silent in the face of harm—she is not too much. She is awake. A girl who dreams of changing the world, who pours her heart into her art, who feels love with her entire being—she is not too much. She is alive.

If you've been told you are "too much," I invite you to ask yourself: Who benefits when I believe that? Who gains when I shrink? And who suffers when I stop showing up fully?

Because your voice—your presence—was never the problem. The problem is a world still learning how to honor women who refuse to be small.

Reclaiming Your Light

This chapter is not about becoming someone new. It's about returning—returning to the truth of who you were before the world told you to tone it down. Before shame crept in. Before you learned to dim your light just to fit into shadows.

As children, we all began with wonder and freedom. We danced without music. Asked questions without fear. Dreamed without limits. That version of you still lives within you. She may be buried under years of trying to fit in—but she is not gone. She is waiting.

To awaken is not to become. It is to remember. To remember your fire. Your tenderness. Your brilliance.

Your Emotions Are Not Excess

Have you been told you feel too deeply? That your tears come too easily? That your empathy is excessive?

Here's the truth: your emotions are wisdom. They are signals. They are the language of a soul that hasn't shut down.

In a world that rewards numbness and detachment, your capacity to feel is sacred. Let yourself cry. Let yourself laugh until your belly aches. Let yourself scream when injustice strikes. Let it rise. Let it move. Let it breathe.

You are not a burden. You are a wellspring. And the world is parched for your kind of truth.

Letting Go of Shame and Embracing Vulnerability

At the root of the "too much" narrative is often shame—the sense that who we are, in our natural state, is somehow wrong. But shame is not your truth. It is the echo of someone else's fear projected onto your freedom. It is what we feel when we believe love must be earned through smallness.

Real belonging doesn't come from being less. It comes from being real. It arrives when you stop performing and start showing up as you are: whole, raw, luminous, and unfiltered.

Yes, that kind of vulnerability is terrifying. But it is also where true joy lives. When you stop hiding, you make space for relationships, dreams, and healing that can only be found on the other side of courage.

The Power of Presence

The antidote to shame is presence. Not just physical presence, but emotional, spiritual, soul-deep presence. Can you be with yourself without needing to fix anything? Can you sit with your light without apology? Can you hold your full experience—without judgment?

Presence is not performance. It's the quiet choice to stop running from your own depth. And when you do—when you truly anchor into the present—you discover something remarkable: You have always been enough. Not because of what you achieve. Not because you've been approved of. But because you exist.

A Soul That Refuses to Shrink

To the girl who's been told she is "too much," here is your invitation:

Be more. Be louder, if that's your truth. Be softer, if that's your rhythm. Be wild. Be tender. Be quiet. Be fierce. Be messy. Be whole. Be you.

Take up space in rooms that never expected your voice. Wear what makes you feel like yourself. Speak your truth, even when your voice trembles. Laugh loudly. Rest deeply. Overflow.

This is not rebellion. This is reclamation.

You are not here to fit in. You are here to fill the room with your light.

A Final Story: When I Finally Stopped Shrinking

There was a time when I believed my dreams were too big. I feared taking up space in rooms that weren't built for girls like me. So I stayed quiet. I over-explained. I apologized.

But then I met a mentor who saw straight through the fear. She looked me in the eyes and said, *"You were born for this. Stop editing your brilliance."*

That moment cracked something open. I started walking taller. I stopped apologizing for my voice. I let myself take up space. I began to overflow.

And it changed everything.

A Love Letter to the Girl Inside

There is a girl within you—brilliant and bold—who never asked the world for permission to be herself. She only asked to be loved as she is. And she still lives inside you, waiting to be invited forward. She remembers your magic. She remembers your freedom. And she will rise again when you stop asking, "Am I too much?" and start declaring, "I am more than enough."

You do not need someone to give you permission. But if it helps— let this be your moment.

You are not too much.
You are magnificent.
Overflow, beloved.

Not someday.
Now.

With all my heart,
Someone who believes in your light

Tools for the Journey:
You Are Here to Overflow

There comes a moment in every journey when the invitation is no longer to be smaller, safer, or more palatable—but to become more of who you already are. Wholeness is not found in quieting your joy, shrinking your brilliance, or taming your truth. It is found in the holy act of expansion.

You were never meant to be manageable. You were meant to be magnetic. And every part of you that once felt "too much" is the very part of you the world is quietly waiting for.

These tools are not instructions for containment. They are reminders of your design: to overflow. With light. With purpose. With fierce tenderness. Your presence was never a disruption—it was always a declaration.

Rewrite the Story That Tried to Silence You

The world may have handed you a script: Be smaller. Be softer. Be less. But that story was written by those who did not know how to hold your fire. You get to write a new one. A story where your laughter is not too loud—it is joy erupting. Where your ambition is not too bold—it is a signpost of purpose. Where your feelings are not too much—they are a sacred sensitivity, tuned to truth. Reclaim your voice from their limitations. Speak as if your soul is listening. Because it is.

Let Yourself Take Up Space

There is power in being fully expressed. Not performative. Not excessive. Just... real. Try moving through one day without shrinking. Wear the color that makes you feel alive. Say the thing you have been holding back. Take up the full seat at the table. Your bigness is not about domination—it is about liberation. And every time you choose to expand rather than contract, you remind the world: freedom is possible.

Honor the Fear—and Then Rise Anyway

It makes sense that you fear rejection. The wound of being "too much" often begins in love that felt conditional. But you are not that child anymore, negotiating for belonging. Now, you get to choose what stays near your light. You are allowed to let go of anyone who asks you to shrink. Not because they are bad—but because you are growing. The right people will never be threatened by your fullness. They will bow to it in reverence.

Reclaim the Sacredness of Wanting

Your desires were never a burden. They are blueprints. There is no shame in wanting a life that feels expansive, honest, and joyful. Let yourself want with your whole heart. Write down what you long for—not just what is reasonable. Let desire move you forward, not hold you back. Your passion is not a fire to tame—it is a torch to carry.

Practice Presence, Not Performance

You do not have to hustle for visibility. Your existence is already worthy of attention. Instead of striving to prove your value, slow down and feel your breath. Light a candle and let your thoughts soften. Be here—not to impress, but to inhabit. Your radiance is not a result of productivity. It is a quiet glow that comes from being rooted in your truth.

Redefine Power Through Integration

You are allowed to be fierce and gentle. Grounded and fiery. Thoughtful and bold. Strength is not one-note. It is harmony. Give yourself permission to hold contradictions. You are not messy—you are multifaceted. You are not too much—you are a mosaic. Integration is where your power lives. Not in the parts you perform, but in the ones you bring home.

Lead by Overflowing, Not Shrinking

Your light might unsettle those still hiding from theirs. Let it. Your fullness is not an offense—it is a revolution. When you show up in all of who you are, you awaken others to their own potential. This is what sacred leadership looks like: not control, but courage. Not conformity, but embodiment. Keep showing up. Keep being seen. Not for applause—but for truth.

A Final Whisper to Carry

Beloved, you were never meant to be quieted. You were meant to echo. To pulse. To rise like a tide and soften like dusk. You are not too much. You are abundance made visible. Let your presence be a prayer. Let your truth be an offering. Let your overflow be a blessing. You are not here to fit. You are here to fill—spaces, hearts, and futures—with everything only you can bring.

You are not too much.
You are more than enough.
And you are just getting started.

CHAPTER 11

To the Girl Who Wants to Change the World —

Your fire is needed.

There is a spark in you that refuses to dim, no matter how heavy the world becomes. You feel the weight of injustice in your bones. You notice what others overlook. You cry when you hear the news. You imagine a world where kindness is currency, where dignity is not earned—but honored as a birthright.

And maybe they've told you to calm down. To be more realistic. To stop caring so much. But let me tell you the truth that others may have forgotten: that fire inside you is not a flaw. It is a gift. It is sacred. It is a light that was never meant to be dimmed.

You were not born to look away. You were not born to settle. You were not born to blend in. You were born to bring change. To reimagine systems. To ask the hard questions. To hold both heartbreak and hope. To love with such sincerity that the world cannot help but soften in your presence.

Changing the world does not always look like headlines or stages. Sometimes, it looks like sitting beside someone in their pain. It looks like planting seeds you may never see bloom. It looks like standing in quiet rooms where no one else is willing to speak truth—and doing it anyway.

You are not too much for this world. You are exactly what it needs. Your compassion, your curiosity, your rage, your ideas, your tenderness—all of it matters.

But here is what I want you to remember as you carry this fire: protect it. Tend to it. Do not let the apathy of the world steal your warmth. Rest when you need to. Step back when you must. Let others carry the torch with you.

Changing the world is not a solo act. It is a choir of courageous hearts—each voice singing its truth, each life lighting the path a little further.

So keep going, love.

Let your voice tremble, and still speak.

Let your dreams stretch beyond reason, and still believe.

Let your heart break, and still return to love.

The world is shifting because you are in it.

And the fire you carry?
It is lighting the way.

With all my heart,
Someone who believes in your fire.

Life Lesson:
You Were Born to Lead With Love

Your Fire Is Needed

There is something extraordinary about a girl who looks at a hurting world and still believes she can be part of its healing. This chapter is for the girl who dreams big, who burns bright, and who dares to care deeply—even when it feels too heavy. You might not always have the right words, the full plan, or the support you deserve—but your fire, your voice, and your courage are needed more than ever.

I have known this fire. It began as a whisper in my chest when I was still a child—when war broke my world apart, when safety vanished, and when I learned that silence was often a survival strategy. But even then, I knew I wanted to make things better. I wanted to protect others the way I wished I had been protected. I wanted to speak the words others were afraid to say. I wanted to create beauty in places where everything felt broken.

That desire never left me. It followed me through refugee camps, through resettlement, through classrooms where I was the only girl of color, through years of hiding parts of myself just to survive. Even in the hardest seasons, it flickered quietly within me. A tiny light. A quiet reminder that I was meant to be more than what had happened to me.

If you are reading this and thinking, *"But who am I to change the world?"*—I want to pause you right there.

You are exactly the kind of person who can change it.

Because real world-changers are not always the loudest in the room. They are not necessarily the ones with the biggest platforms or the fanciest degrees. They are the ones who are willing to begin. To show up. To care. Even when the odds are stacked against them.

You see, wanting to make a difference isn't naïve—it's necessary. And your fire? It doesn't make you too much. It makes you luminous.

The Cost of Caring

Caring deeply in an indifferent world can sometimes feel like a burden. Maybe you've been told to "calm down," "stop being dramatic," or "let it go." Maybe you've been asked why you care so much about things that "aren't your problem."

But the world does not change through indifference. It transforms because of people like you—those who refuse to look away, who ask the uncomfortable questions, who show up when no one else will.

Still, caring can be exhausting. You may find yourself pouring out and rarely being poured into. You may lose sleep over causes that seem too big to solve. You may wonder if your voice is loud enough to matter.

In those moments, come back to this truth: your fire doesn't need to be a wildfire to be real. Even a steady flame can light the way for others. You do not need to fix everything. You only need to keep choosing to care, to speak, to act—in your way, in your time.

The Tension Between Hope and Heartbreak

Changing the world is not a fairytale. It involves disappointment, resistance, and moments of heartbreak. You will see injustice that feels immovable. You will witness suffering you cannot undo. You will encounter people who do not want to listen.

But you will also witness small miracles. A girl who finds her voice. A community that rises together. A door that opens for someone who was once left outside.

This is the paradox of activism and compassion—holding both the ache and the hope. Allowing yourself to be cracked open by the pain of the world, while still believing in its possibility.

Let your heartbreak become holy. Let it teach you how to love more fiercely, not less. Let it shape you into someone who leads with tenderness, who refuses to become hardened.

Reclaiming the Right to Dream

Too many girls are taught that dreaming is a luxury. That their job is to survive, not to imagine. That big visions are for someone else.

But dreaming is not a distraction from reality. It is a form of resistance. It is how we imagine new realities. It is how we remember what we are capable of.

So dream. Dream unapologetically. Whether you want to build a school, run for office, start a movement, or raise a kind family—your dreams are valid. Your desires are worthy.

Let yourself dream without asking for permission. Let your future be shaped by purpose, not fear. And remember, your dreams do not have to look like anyone else's to be powerful.

Fire Without Burnout

Let us be honest: changing the world is a long journey. And no one can run on fire forever. That is why it is essential to tend to your flame with care.

You do not have to be "on" all the time. You do not have to prove your commitment through exhaustion. In fact, one of the most radical things you can do is to take care of your spirit.

Build rhythms that nourish you. Create rituals that restore your hope. Surround yourself with people who reflect your light back to you when you forget it is there.

Rest is not quitting. Rest is wisdom.

Remembering Where You Come From

Sometimes the fire dims. Sometimes doubt creeps in. In those moments, I return to my roots.

I remember the girl who prayed in a tent after fleeing war. I remember the girl who translated for her parents, carried water for miles, and still held onto joy. I remember that version of me— and I honor her.

You have those versions of yourself, too. The girl who kept going. The girl who dared to hope. The girl who spoke up even when her voice trembled.

She is still within you. She is still guiding you.

You Are Part of Something Bigger

The world may try to make you feel small. But the truth is: you are part of a lineage of change-makers. You are not the first girl to feel this fire, and you will not be the last.

Every time you choose love over fear, every time you stand tall instead of shrinking, every time you bring light to a dark place— you join hands with millions of girls, women, and allies who are shaping the future with grace and grit.

This is the movement. And you are a part of it.

So take up space. Speak with courage. Use your fire to ignite others.

The world may not change overnight—but every time you show up, you help it shift.

Keep going.
Your fire is needed.
Your voice matters.
And your dream is already making a difference.

Tools for the Journey:
Lead With Love and Purpose

Changing the world is not about perfection. It is about presence. And presence begins with understanding that the fire in you—your longing to create something better, more beautiful, more just—is not too big. It is sacred.

This chapter is for every girl who has ever felt like she is carrying the weight of the world on her shoulders. For every dreamer, activist, artist, healer, and everyday soul who believes that something better is possible. You are not here by accident. You are here on purpose—with purpose.

But sometimes, the path of changemaking can feel heavy. Exhausting. Lonely. You may start to question whether your efforts matter, or if you are asking too much of the world—or even of yourself.

Let this be your gentle reminder: the fire within you is not meant to burn you out—it is meant to light the way. These tools are here to help you stay connected to that light, without losing yourself in the process.

Anchor Before You Act

Before rushing to change the world, take time to anchor in your own presence. Ground yourself. Root in who you are.

Ask yourself: *What am I connected to? Why does this matter to me?*

This simple pause helps you respond from alignment, not urgency. A still, rooted heart can hold a powerful fire without being consumed by it.

Practice Daily Renewal

Change is not sustained by adrenaline. It is sustained by devotion. And devotion needs rest.

Give yourself permission to take breaks, to unplug, to play. Let joy be part of your activism. Let your body rest. The most enduring revolutions are built on rhythms of renewal.

Create small, sacred daily practices that fill you back up:

- Five minutes of silence
- A warm morning drink
- A walk with no destination
- Laughter with someone you trust

You do not need to earn rest. You need to embody it.

Choose Integrity Over Approval

World-changers often face resistance. Not everyone will understand your vision, your passion, or your fire.

Do it anyway.

Let your values guide you more than applause. Choose integrity even when it's unpopular. The quiet confidence of living in alignment with your truth will nourish you more deeply than the fleeting high of validation.

Ask yourself often: *Does this align with my values?*

Not: *Will they approve of me if I do this?*

Do Not Carry the World Alone

It is tempting to believe you must do it all. That if you just gave more, loved more, worked harder—everything would be fixed.

But change is a collective journey. You were never meant to carry it all by yourself.

Find your people. Your co-dreamers. Your soul family. Those who remind you that your fire is sacred—and that your rest is sacred, too.

Let yourself receive support. Ask for help. Be honest about what you need. You do not have to earn belonging. You simply have to allow it.

Let Small Be Sacred

Changing the world does not always look like grand gestures. Sometimes it looks like:

- The kindness you extend to a stranger
- The boundaries you hold
- The truth you speak in a quiet room

Small things ripple. Consistency is powerful. Presence is enough.

You do not need to go viral to make a difference. You just need to stay rooted in what is real, true, and meaningful to you.

Grieve and Rise

The journey of world-changing will bring grief. You will see injustice. You will lose hope. You will face burnout. It is okay to feel that. It is okay to grieve.

But do not grieve alone.

Let your tears be part of your healing. Let them water the ground where your courage grows. Let sorrow move through you—then let it shape your compassion, not harden your heart.

Grieving is not weakness. It is evidence of your capacity to love.

CHAPTER 12

To the Girl With Big Dreams But No Support —

Your dream chose you for a reason.

I see you—sitting with a heart full of ideas, visions, and longings that feel too big for the world you're standing in. You look around and realize that no one seems to get it. Maybe they tell you to be more "realistic." Maybe they smile politely when you speak of your hopes. Or maybe they say nothing at all—just silence, like your dreams don't even exist.

But let me say this as clearly as I can: your dream is not an accident. It is not too big. It is not asking too much. It is sacred. And it chose you for a reason.

You may not have the mentors, the funding, the connections, or the cheerleaders right now. But you have something else—something just as powerful. You have vision. You have resilience. You have a soul that dares to imagine more than what you were handed.

Sometimes, the people around you cannot support your dream because they've never seen what you see. It's not their fault. They haven't been called to it—you have. That's why the fire is in your chest, not theirs.

And I know—it's hard. To hold a dream with both hands and still feel alone. To speak life into something that no one else seems to hear. To walk forward not knowing if anyone will ever walk beside you. But that doesn't make your dream less worthy. If anything, it means you are walking the road most don't have the courage to choose.

So keep going.

Even if you start small. Even if your voice shakes. Even if you have to learn everything from scratch. Even if the only one who believes in it today is you.

Because one day—whether in a room full of people who finally understand or in the quiet of your own becoming—you will look back and realize: you didn't need permission to dream. You only needed the courage to trust the seed inside you.

And you already have that.

With love and belief,
Someone who kept going too.

Life Lesson:
Your Dream Chose You for a Reason

Some of us are born with dreams that feel too big for the rooms we grow up in. We are the ones who looked out the window and saw something more—not because we were ungrateful for what we had, but because something within us whispered: *There's more to this life. And you're meant to help shape it.*

If this is you, this chapter is for you.

I was one of those girls. As a child, even in the middle of war, even as a refugee, I dreamed of speaking on global stages, advocating for children, and helping change the world. I didn't have a roadmap. I had questions. I had hunger. I had hope.

And often, I felt alone.

When you have big dreams and no support, it can feel like standing at the edge of a cliff—knowing you're meant to leap, but with no one behind you to say, "Go. I believe in you."

Maybe you know what that's like. Maybe you've had moments where your dream felt foolish. Where you were told you were reaching too far, aiming too high. Or worse—maybe no one said anything, and their silence became the loudest kind of discouragement.

But here's what I want you to know: some dreams are too sacred to be understood by everyone. Some dreams arrive as whispers only *you* can hear. And it's not your job to convince others of their worth. It's your job to honor them. To nourish them. To say yes, even when no one else does.

The Loneliness of Vision

Visionaries often walk alone—especially in the beginning. The dreamers, the artists, the activists, the builders—so many of them began in quiet places, doubted by those closest to them.

Why? Because to dream is to stretch the imagination. To disrupt the status quo. And that can make people uncomfortable—especially those who've learned to survive by staying small.

But dreaming isn't about ego. It's about alignment. It's about recognizing the part of you that already belongs to the future you're trying to create. And when you feel out of place in your surroundings, it doesn't mean you're wrong. It may mean you're evolving.

There is nothing wrong with being the first to see it. There is nothing wrong with carrying a dream no one claps for yet. Let that be your quiet revolution.

Dreaming Amidst Scarcity

There were years when all I had was a notebook and my voice. There were no investors. No guaranteed outcomes. Just a girl who had survived war, carried too much sorrow, and still believed that love could be louder.

What kept me going? Faith. Not in systems. Not in luck. But in the unshakable truth that my dream chose me for a reason.

And maybe that's what will carry you too.

If you are the girl with big dreams but no support, you are not alone—you are early. You are ahead. You are the beginning of a new chapter, one that generations may one day look back on and thank you for writing.

Listening to the Voice Within

There will be external voices—loud ones—telling you to choose what is safe, proven, predictable. But the voice that matters most is the quiet one within. The one that says: *Keep going.*

Listen to that voice.

There were times I doubted myself. Times I failed. Times I cried because I couldn't see how it would all work out. But not once did I stop showing up. Not once did I let go of the dream completely.

Because every time I thought about quitting, I remembered why I started: for the little girl who survived, for the women who felt voiceless, for the communities who deserved more.

And you? Your reason is just as worthy.

Redefining Support

Sometimes we think support must look a certain way—a mentor, a sponsor, a cheerleader. And while those are powerful, they're not the only kinds of support.

Support can be:

- A journal where you pour your hopes.

- A quiet friend who sees your heart.

- A teacher who says, "I see something in you."

- A moment of stillness where you feel connected to something bigger.

You don't need an audience to begin. You need truth. You need belief. You need the courage to say, *Even if no one shows up—I will.*

Growing Through Rejection

Rejection doesn't always mean the dream isn't right. Sometimes it's redirection. Sometimes it's refinement. Sometimes it's just a test to see how deeply you're willing to believe.

Each "no" I've ever received taught me something:

- How to be clear in my vision.

- How to advocate for myself.

- How to find people who actually align with my purpose.

So if you've been told no—if you've been dismissed or overlooked—do not shrink. Let it strengthen you. Let it teach you what your "yes" must feel like.

Letting the Dream Change You

The most powerful dreams are not just about what we build—but about who we become in the process.

Dreaming is not only about success. It is about transformation. It is about healing the parts of you that were told you weren't enough. It's about choosing to show up in your fullness again and again because you believe the world is better with your light in it.

Your dream is not a destination. It is a relationship—one that asks for your presence, your trust, your willingness to be shaped.

Holding the Dream Gently

There will be seasons when your dream feels far away. That's okay. Let it rest. Let it breathe. Some things bloom in silence.

Return to it when you're ready. Trust that it will still be there. Dreams are patient. They know the way home.

And if life pulls you into detours—caring for others, healing, surviving—that doesn't mean your dream has died. It means your roots are deepening. It means your future will stand taller.

Awakening to Your Enoughness

At the heart of every big dream is a quiet question: *Am I enough to carry this?*

And the answer is: Yes, love. You are.

Not because you're perfect. But because you're willing.
Because you care.
Because you're brave enough to hope.

And that, in itself, changes the world.

So hold your dream close. Speak life into it. Take one small step—even when the path is unclear.

You were never too much. You have always been enough.
And your dream? It knew exactly who to choose.

You.

Let's keep walking.
Let's build what we've never seen.
Let's rise.

Tools for the Journey:
Nurture the Vision That Chose You

Some dreams do not arrive with fanfare. They come in whispers— in quiet nudges that return no matter how many times you question them. They ask you to believe before there is evidence. To begin before there is applause.

And the truth is, the most powerful dreams often come to those without a map, a mentor, or a cheering crowd. Not because you are unworthy of support—but because your soul was strong enough to carry something others may not yet understand.

You were not chosen for your certainty.

You were chosen for your willingness to believe.

Let these tools be gentle companions as you learn to trust what only you can see.

Return to the Whisper Within

The dream that lives in you is not random. It found you—because something in your spirit, your story, your voice is meant to bring it to life. When the outside world is quiet or even doubting, turn inward. Let your own breath become your anchor. Light a candle. Sit with a journal. Walk without distraction. Ask: *What part of me still believes?* Listen closely. That voice inside may be small, but it is sacred.

Take Micro-Steps with Devotion

You do not need to leap to be faithful. You only need to move. One sentence written. One email sent. One idea spoken aloud. These small steps are not insignificant—they are sacred acts of devotion. They tell the universe: *I am here. I am still listening.* Build slowly. But build. Even without applause. Especially without applause.

Build a Circle That Reflects Possibility

Sometimes the most painful part of dreaming is doing it alone. But support can be built—even if it must begin with strangers. Seek out voices that affirm you. Books, podcasts, online communities, distant mentors. Gather with people who fan your flame, not dim it. Even one aligned soul can shift the entire landscape of your becoming.

Let Doubt Teach You, Not Silence You

Doubt is not a sign you are lost. It is a sign you are on sacred ground. Let it ask its questions—but do not let it steal your voice. When fear rises, ask: *What would it mean to believe in my dream fully—even just for today?* Do not wait for certainty to begin. Let courage lead, even in uncertainty.

See Loneliness as Sacred Preparation

The ache of walking alone is real—but so is the refining that happens there. When no one else sees your dream, you begin to see it more clearly yourself. You learn to trust your own vision, to strengthen your own voice. What you are cultivating in private will one day bless someone else in public. This is the soil where roots grow.

Become the One Who Claps First

Validation does not always come from others. Sometimes, it must come from within. Write love notes to your own tenacity. Speak your own name with reverence. Track your progress, even when it feels invisible. Tell yourself: *This matters. I matter. I am building something real.* Because you are. And you always have been.

Let Rest Be Part of the Rhythm

Carrying a dream alone can be exhausting. But burnout is not the badge of bravery. Rest is. Rest means you trust that your dream is still growing, even in your stillness. It means you care enough to preserve the vessel carrying the vision. Rest without apology. Your pause is not your failure—it is your faith.

Refuse to Inherit Their Limits

Not everyone will see what you see. Some will project their fear onto your dream and call it realism. But you are not here to carry their limitations. You are here to write new stories. Whisper new possibilities. Break old patterns. Just because no one around you has done it, does not mean you cannot.

Their disbelief is not a prophecy.
Your vision is not a mistake.
Keep going.

A Final Word to Carry

You may be the only one who sees the path right now. That does not make it any less real. Because some of the most world-shifting things began in silence. In solitude. In the heart of someone brave enough to believe anyway. Your dream chose you for a reason. Tend to it. Speak to it. Walk with it. Even when no one is watching. Especially then. You do not need to be certain. You only need to begin. And you already have.

From One Heart to Another —
Quiet Power, Bold Legacy *Letter from a champion*

Mi Carmen,

There's a photograph I keep—of you, fresh from the pool, droplets clinging to your chest, your face tilted slightly to the sky in a way that says: I belong here. Even then, you held your space with quiet certainty. You weren't small—not in presence, not in spirit. You were already whole.

It's funny—I used to think I was raising you, but more and more, I realize: you've been teaching me, too.

You are my fish, my old soul. You move through life with the same quiet force I see in the water—steady, deep, never rushed, but always arriving. I see it in how you wake before the sun, slipping into cold pools not just to swim, but to perform. You push your body into choreography that demands the strength of an athlete and the precision of a dancer. You rise from the water not just graceful, but powerful—part discipline, part poetry. You turn effort into beauty. You make hard things look like grace.

And then there's the part of you that retreats—curled up in a corner, book in hand, lost to another world. Or hunched over your notebook late at night, guitar resting beside you, writing songs no one asked for but the world quietly needs. That quiet fire inside you—that's where your leadership lives. Not in volume or spotlight, but in truth. In creation. In your unwavering commitment to being deeply, beautifully yourself.

You are a symphony of opposites. Gentle, but strong. Quiet, yet unwavering. Aloof, but deeply engaged. A dreamer and a doer. A child who has never been just a child, always somehow older than your years, as if you've lived lifetimes before this one.

Sometimes you follow, and that's okay. Sometimes you sit at the edge, observing. But I see the leader in you—not the one who commands the room, but the one who creates space for others to grow. True leadership isn't about being in front—it's about lifting others alongside you. And I see that in you: how you support your teammates, how you cheer on your friends, how you make room for others to shine. You don't need to be louder to be heard. You don't need to be bigger to matter. Never mistake your softness for weakness. Your tenderness is your power.

You come from people who did the impossible—twice. Tito, my father, arrived in Canada as a trained veterinarian, but had to start over—selling gas contracts door-to-door, not because it was easy, but because it was necessary. For seven years, he studied, rewrote exams, failed some, passed others—and never gave up. Eventually, he did it: he became a certified veterinarian in Canada, too.

Nanny, my mother—once a respected teacher in Mexico—also started again. She cleaned houses, worked cash registers, and, in her late forties, returned to school in a second language to become a lab technician. Together, they rebuilt their veterinary hospital—first in Mexico, then again in Canada. Two lives. One love. And a resilience that built the foundation beneath us all.

There is no Tito without Nanny. No Nanny without Tito. They are two halves of a beautiful whole—not just in love, but in purpose. Their story isn't one of overnight success, but of showing up again and again, even when it was hard. They failed. They started over. They leaned on each other. And they never gave up. That's the legacy you carry: strength not just in achievement, but in perseverance. In humility. In building something that lasts—even when no one is watching, even when no one claps. Let their story remind you: the most meaningful things in life are rarely fast or easy, but they are always worth the effort.

And then there's your dad, Shawn. Your softness lives in him, too. The two of you share a secret language built from board games, character sheets, Dungeons & Dragons campaigns, and joyful silliness. You're both kids at heart, meeting in that sacred place where imagination runs free. I watch you giggle together over things I don't quite understand, and it fills me with warmth. He understands your quiet—not as distance, but as depth. He holds space for your gentleness without ever asking you to change.

And Nico—your big brother, your compass in a world that doesn't always make sense. He has always seen you. Truly seen you. Even before the rest of us could name what made you so extraordinary, he understood you with a glance. You were the first person he trusted with his truth, and you held it with the care only a sister like you could offer. The two of you are yin and yang: his fire, your water; his voice, your calm. Where he is bold and social, you are observant and still— but together, you are whole. Watching you both is like witnessing a conversation without words. He draws you out. You center him. You bring out each other's softness, playfulness, and strength. That kind of bond is rare, mi amor. Protect it. Nurture it. It is one of the great loves of your life.

And me? We have our own rhythm, don't we? The long talks on your bed. The slow mornings getting dressed. Picking out earrings that feel like tiny acts of joy. We don't always need words. Sometimes, just being beside you—breathing the same air, sharing the same silence—fills my soul in ways nothing else can.

And then there are our car rides—long stretches of road to your competitions, filled with rom-com audiobooks, girly playlists, and the comfort of just being together. We've made a ritual of food adventures too—trying dishes we can't pronounce, ordering whatever sounds the most unfamiliar, enjoying sauces and spices from places we dream of visiting. In those moments—between bites, between songs, between stories—I feel closest to you. You are my reflection, my lesson, my softness and strength in one.

When the world feels like too much—and sometimes it will—come back to this:
You already carry generations of resilience in your bones.
You are made of melody and muscle, of waves and wonder.
You are both the whisper and the roar.

Don't rush your blooming. Don't dull your shine to fit somewhere smaller. The world will try to name you, box you, hurry you. Let it try. You'll just keep being Carmen.
And that will always be more than enough.

If you see yourself in these pages—quiet, curious, unsure—know this: you're not alone.
This letter is for you, too.

Love,
Mamá

PART V

Heal: Rise, Softly and Again

Healing is not linear. But it is always yours to choose.

There is a quiet truth we come to know, often after loss, rupture, or silence:

Healing is not a destination.

It is a sacred rhythm of returning to ourselves—again and again.

Sometimes with trembling hands. Sometimes with fierce resolve. Always, with love.

This part of the journey is not about fixing what is broken.

It is about remembering what was whole before the wounds.

It is a call to rise gently. To come home to yourself not with urgency, but with grace.

To unlearn the myth that healing must look like perfection—and instead, to trust that softness is still strength. That rest is a form of resistance in a world that demands we keep going even when our souls are asking us to pause.

Here, we release the pressure to have it all figured out.

We honor the seasons of stillness.

We recognize that our deepest power often lives beneath the surface—in the quiet decision to try again. To forgive again. To breathe through the ache. To believe in something more.

You do not need to rush.
You are not behind.
Healing has no timeline.

Whether you are just beginning, returning after a long pause, or walking through the aftermath of a storm you never chose—this part is yours.

An invitation to meet yourself where you are.

To cradle the pieces with tenderness.

And to rise with a softness that does not demand performance—but invites truth.

You are not broken.
You are beautifully becoming.
And you are allowed to rise—softly, and again.

From One Heart to Another — Gratitude in the Becoming   *Letter from a champion*

Dear Girl Who Wonders If Her Struggles Will Ever End,

I see you.

I see the way you carry so much in silence—your questions, your fears, the ache of trying to be enough in a world that keeps asking for more. I know what it feels like to walk through life holding your breath, hoping not to disappoint anyone, and wondering if it is safe to just be yourself. And I want to begin by saying: you are not alone.

If I could sit beside my younger self—the one who often cried quietly behind closed doors, who held her tongue to avoid being misunderstood, who mistook silence for safety—I would not change a single thing about her. I would not take away her struggles, even if I could. And that might surprise you.

Because it was in those very struggles that I found my becoming.

Those hard moments—the ones that made me question my worth, the ones that stretched me beyond what I thought I could bear—became my greatest teachers. They taught me to be grateful. Not in a way that ignores pain or pretends that injustice is okay. But in a way that helps me recognize beauty in unlikely places. In a way that allows my heart to remain soft and open, even in a world that can be harsh and demanding.

Today, my heart is full of gratitude not because my life has been easy, but because I have learned to see even my pain as part of the mosaic that makes me who I am. I wake up each day with a quiet joy for the simple things: a warm conversation, a safe space to just be, the sound of my own laughter returning after a long absence. These are the things that matter. And I learned to cherish them because of what I went through.

But I want to be honest with you. There was a time when I tried to hide the parts of me that felt too messy or complicated. As a child,

I would often hold back. I kept my opinions quiet, swallowed my questions, and tucked away any sadness—because I was afraid of being judged, misunderstood, or seen as a burden. I thought that if I just smiled enough, behaved well enough, said the right things, I would be loved more easily. I thought being "perfect" was the safest way to belong.

Maybe you know that feeling too.

But here is what life eventually taught me—and what I now offer to you with so much love: pretending is not protection. It is a cage. And no matter how polished that cage looks on the outside, it will never feel like home.

I was lucky to learn—through mistakes, heartbreaks, and a few brave choices—that living authentically is the only way to feel truly free. And yes, it can be scary. Yes, some people will misunderstand you. But none of that will matter as much as the deep peace that comes from being fully, honestly you.

When you live a life of honesty, you begin to attract the people and places that were meant for the real you—not the version you curated to please others. You stop feeling like you are performing, and start feeling like you are living. And that, sweet girl, is everything.

So here is what I hope you remember, especially when the world tells you to be smaller, quieter, less complicated:

Let your struggle shape you, but never let it define you.
Let your voice rise, even when it shakes.
Let your truth breathe, even if it is messy.
Let your gratitude soften you, even when life feels hard.
And most of all—let yourself be known. Fully. Tenderly. Truthfully.

Because the honest you is always the best you.

With all my heart,
Carolina

CHAPTER 13

To the Girl Who's Healing in Her Own Time —

You don't have to rush your becoming.

There is no finish line to healing.
No gold medal waiting at the end of your tears.
No perfect version of yourself hidden behind a door you must sprint to open.

There is only this moment—this breath—and the quiet, sacred unfolding of your truth.

I know the pressure to be okay. To look healed.

To speak without trembling. To smile like the past didn't happen. But healing is not a performance. It is not something to prove. It is a transformation that often happens invisibly, slowly, beneath the surface. It is the quiet courage to keep waking up to yourself, even when your heart feels tender, raw, and unfinished.

Some days, you will take five steps forward. Other days, you may feel like you've slipped back into the ache you thought you had already outgrown. That is not failure. That is healing. That is life. And you are allowed to do it at your own pace.

You do not owe anyone a timeline. Not your family. Not your friends. Not even the younger version of you who once whispered, *I hope we're okay by now.* You do not have to rush to make her proud.

You simply have to stay. To be present. To offer her the tenderness she needed then—and still needs now.

If all you did today was breathe—if all you managed was to sit with your feelings without pushing them away—if you cried, or paused, or whispered "I'm trying," That is enough. Because your story is still unfolding, your roots are still growing deeper. Your petals will open in time. And even in the waiting, even in the breaking, even in the soft, slow work of mending—you are becoming.

Let the world rush. Let others chase. But you? You are allowed to move slowly. To rise gently. To heal in your own time.

There is no need to rush your becoming, love. You are healing. And that is more than enough.

With all my heart,
Someone who is still healing too.

Life Lesson:
You Don't Have to Rush Your Becoming

There is a part of us that aches for resolution—for the moment when we can finally say, "I am healed," as if healing is a finish line we will one day reach and be done with. But the truth is, healing is not a single event. It is a tender, spiraling return to ourselves—a process shaped by grace, pauses, and the willingness to meet each version of ourselves along the way with love.

This chapter is for the girl learning to heal—for the one who still flinches when certain memories resurface, who has days when she feels like she is back at the beginning, and who wonders if she'll ever feel whole.

I want you to know: You are not behind. You are not broken. You are learning the sacred rhythm of rising, softly and again.

The Wound That Taught Me to Listen

I remember a time in my life when I thought healing meant forgetting. I wanted to silence the past, to bury the pain beneath layers of productivity and busyness. If I could just stay distracted, I thought, maybe the ache would disappear.

But pain has a way of whispering until it is heard.

Mine showed up in the form of anxiety, burnout, and a deep disconnection from myself. I had spent so long surviving that I forgot what it meant to feel. It wasn't until I slowed down—really slowed down—that I began to listen.

Grief surfaced. Memories returned. And I realized: healing doesn't happen by rushing forward. It happens when we stop running and learn to sit with ourselves in love.

The Myth of Linear Healing

We are told stories of recovery that follow a neat path: pain, then progress, then peace. But most healing journeys are not like that. They are layered, nonlinear, and often filled with returns.

You might feel joy in the morning and grief by sunset. You might have months of stability followed by a wave of unexpected sadness. This does not mean you are failing. It means you are human.

Your nervous system is learning safety. Your soul is learning rest. Your heart is learning trust again.

Healing is not a ladder—it's a spiral. And every time you circle back to an old wound, you are arriving with deeper wisdom and a softer heart.

Allowing Slowness to Be Sacred

In a world that glorifies speed, urgency, and constant achievement, choosing to heal slowly is a revolutionary act.

Slowness allows us to listen—to our bodies, to our needs, to the quiet voice of truth inside us. It teaches us to notice. To breathe. To rest without guilt.

Some days, healing might look like getting out of bed. Other days, it might look like setting a boundary, forgiving yourself, or choosing joy. There is no wrong pace. Your path is your own.

When the Past Returns

You might find yourself revisiting pain you thought you had already released. Old fears may reappear. Grief may reawaken.

This is not regression—it's deepening.

Healing invites us to revisit our stories from new vantage points. To offer our younger selves compassion. To rewrite the narratives we once believed about our worth, our voice, our identity.

With every return, you are more equipped. You are no longer the girl standing in the middle of the storm—you are the woman who has learned how to hold her own hand through it.

The Power of Presence

Healing is not only about what we leave behind—it's about what we learn to embrace.

When we stop rushing toward a future version of ourselves, we begin to witness the beauty of who we are right now. The breath. The heartbeat. The quiet resilience.

Presence is what makes space for peace. And peace is what begins to soften the edges of pain.

You don't need to have it all figured out to be worthy of rest. You don't need to be fully healed to be fully loved.

The Sacred Pause

There will be seasons when growth is invisible. When all you are doing is surviving, breathing, showing up. That is enough.

Healing often happens in the sacred pause—in the rest, in the silence, in the moments no one sees.

Honor these pauses. They are not delays. They are preparation.

Becoming the Safe Place

As you learn to heal, you become the safe place your younger self never had. You learn to speak to yourself with tenderness. To hold your fears with love. To trust your body's signals instead of ignoring them.

You begin to parent yourself with patience. To nourish your spirit with what it needs. To become the home you've always searched for.

This is the quiet miracle of healing—it transforms not only how we see ourselves, but how we show up for others.

A Whisper for the Journey

If today feels heavy, let it be heavy. If you feel tired,
let yourself rest.

You are allowed to take the scenic route. You are allowed to cry in the middle of the climb. You are allowed to be exactly where you are.

Your healing does not need to make sense to anyone else. It does not need to look impressive. It only needs to feel true. You are not behind. You are not too late. You are right on time. You don't have to rush your becoming.

Return to yourself with love. Return again. And again. And again.

That is healing. That is enough.

Tools for the Journey:
Trust the Pace of Your Own Healing

Healing is not something to conquer. It is something to be in relationship with. We are taught to race toward outcomes, to measure our growth by speed, milestones, or how little we seem to need. But real healing is not efficient—it is intimate. It unfolds in spirals, not straight lines. It asks for presence, not performance.

These tools are not tasks for self-improvement. They are invitations to return to the sacred rhythm of becoming—one that moves at the pace of trust, not urgency. If you have ever felt behind, broken, or afraid that your softness makes you weak, may these words remind you: *you are allowed to heal slowly.* You are allowed to rise gently. And you are allowed to be in the middle of your becoming and still be worthy of love.

Trust the Rhythm That Holds You

You are not late to your own life. The world may praise fast transformations, but you are allowed to grow slowly. Healing does not always feel like progress. Sometimes it feels like stillness. Like grief. Like sitting in silence with the ache that won't move. But even in that quiet, you are becoming.

There is a pace within you that knows exactly what is sustainable. Let it lead.

Choose Grace Over Shame

Shame will tell you that you are failing because you are still healing. That you should be "better" by now. But shame is not truth. It is the echo of voices that demanded your perfection before they offered you compassion.

.Practice speaking to yourself with tenderness, not judgment. Try whispering: *It is okay to still be learning. It is okay to not have it all figured out. I am still worthy—especially here.*

Practice the Sacredness of Small Healing

Healing doesn't only happen in breakthroughs. It happens in micro-moments that often go unnoticed:

– Choosing to rest instead of proving your strength.
– Letting tears fall without rushing to stop them.
– Making a nourishing meal, even when your heart is heavy.
– Laughing for the first time in a long time.

These are not small things. They are acts of courage that say: *I am still here. I am still trying. I am still choosing life.*

Release Perfection as a Requirement for Love

Perfection is often the mask we wear to feel safe. If I am perfect, maybe they will not leave. Maybe I will finally belong. But perfectionism is not protection—it is distance. It asks you to abandon your messy, beautiful humanity in exchange for approval.

Let go. Let your softness lead. Let your flaws breathe. Let your healing be witnessed in its rawness, not its polish. You are already enough.

Create Rituals of Gentle Return

Rituals remind your nervous system that safety is possible. That healing is not a destination, but a rhythm of returning.

Try lighting a candle and placing a hand over your heart. Whisper something true, even if it hurts. Write down one thing you survived today. Let these quiet rituals become the steady ground beneath you. They are not performance. They are presence.

Let Yourself Be Witnessed Without Being Fixed

You don't need a crowd. But you do need kind witnesses—those who see your slow unfolding and do not ask you to hurry. Whether it is a therapist, a friend, a mentor, or the words of someone who walked this road before you—let yourself be supported.

Let them hold space without trying to mend you. You are not broken. You are blooming at your own pace.

Rebuild Trust With Your Inner Knowing

There is a voice within you that remembers who you were before the world told you to rush. A voice that doesn't shout, but gently guides.

When you feel lost, return to your breath. When you feel overwhelmed, place your feet on the ground. Ask: *What do I know to be true in this moment?* Not forever. Just now.

This is how you learn to hear yourself again—not all at once, but breath by breath.

A Final Whisper to Carry

You do not have to rush your healing to prove your worth.
You do not have to finish your becoming to deserve rest.
You are allowed to rise slowly, with softness and grace.
You are allowed to heal out loud—and in silence.
You are allowed to bloom quietly, at your own pace.

This is not failure. This is fidelity—to your soul, your story, and your sacred timing.

You are healing. You are becoming. And that, beloved, is more than enough.

CHAPTER 14

To the Girl Who Feels Like She'll Never Be Whole Again —

Wholeness is not what you lost. It is what you rebuild.

I see you.

Sitting in the quiet, holding the shattered pieces of something that once felt whole. Maybe it was your childhood. Maybe it was your sense of safety. Maybe it was the belief that life would always make sense. Whatever it was—when it broke, something inside you cracked open, too.

And now, you are here. Trying to make sense of the ache. Wondering if you will ever feel like yourself again. Wondering if there is even a self to return to.

But love, please know this: wholeness is not about never having been broken. It is not about erasing the pain or pretending the wounds were never there. It is about the love you gather as you rebuild. The grace you offer to every fractured part. The way you learn to carry what once tried to break you—with softness, with dignity, with care.

You do not have to go back to who you were before the hurt. That version of you hadn't yet walked through fire. She hadn't yet discovered the strength of her own breath, the resilience of her spirit, or the quiet, fierce tenderness that now lives in your bones.

You are not broken beyond repair. You are a mosaic in the making. And every scar, every tear, every soft return to yourself is part of the masterpiece. Even the cracks can hold light.

Some days, healing will feel like blooming. Other days, it will feel like simply surviving. But even in the stillness—even in the not-yet—you are becoming. You are not behind. You are not lost. You are in the sacred process of remembering who you are beneath what happened.

And you are not alone in this.

Many of us have walked through fire and come out whispering truth with ash-stained hands. We've mourned what could have been. We've questioned whether we would ever feel whole again. And in our quiet, we stand beside you—heart to heart, breath to breath—reminding you that healing does not mean forgetting. It means choosing to keep becoming.

There is no rush. No test to pass. No finish line to reach. Only this: the tender, persistent invitation to rebuild at your own pace, to gather each piece with gentleness, and to trust that you are being made new—not despite your pain, but through it.

So when it feels like too much, when the grief swells louder than hope, please hold on to this: you are not starting from nothing. You are starting from everything you survived.

Wholeness is not a return. It is a re-creation. And your heart already knows how to begin again.

With all my love,
Someone who believes you are already enough.

Life Lesson:
Wholeness Is What You Rebuild

I used to think wholeness was something you either had or didn't. That once life fractured you—through loss, betrayal, war, abandonment, or grief—there was no returning. That healing would only ever mean learning to carry the pieces.

But I know better now.

Because I have lived with the ache of being shattered. I have sat inside the silence of prayers that went unanswered. I have cried into pillows I didn't own, slept in rooms that didn't remember me, and wondered if my heart would ever feel like home again. And somehow—through the smallest steps and the slowest kindnesses—I began to rebuild.

The Day My World Split in Two

There is a moment etched in my memory like a scar on stone.

I was just a girl, walking home with a warm meal in my hand and laughter still lingering from that morning. I didn't know it would be the last time I'd see home as I knew it. Conflict broke open around us like thunder, and the life we'd built collapsed overnight.

One day, I belonged to a village. The next, I belonged to no one and nothing but survival.

In the weeks that followed, I went from sleeping in a familiar bed to sharing a refugee tent with strangers. From being called by my name to being called "one of them." From having dreams about the future to trying to forget that I had one.

There is something terrifying about watching the story of your life change mid-sentence—and not knowing if you'll ever get to write the next chapter. And yet, I did. But I didn't do it all at once.

Wholeness Isn't a Return—It's a Becoming

There is a myth we carry, often unconsciously: that healing should bring us back to who we were. But what if who we were wasn't safe? What if that girl had never known stability, or unconditional love, or rest?

What if healing doesn't take us back—it brings us forward?

What I've learned over years of learning to breathe again is this: wholeness is not a perfect restoration. It is a becoming. A re-gathering of our spirit. A return to our true essence—not the one shaped by pain, but the one shaped by love.

Your wholeness might look different than you imagined. It might be softer. Quieter. Slower. But it will be yours.

The Invisible Grief We Carry

One of the greatest weights in the healing process is the grief that goes unacknowledged. Not just grief over people we lost—but grief over who we were before we were hurt. Grief over childhoods that weren't safe. Over friendships that ended without closure. Over dreams that were abandoned just to make room for survival.

So many girls and women I've met around the world carry grief silently. Especially those who had to grow up too soon. Especially those who come from war, from displacement, from generational trauma or the quiet erosion of self-worth through years of being dismissed, silenced, or ignored.

If you've ever wondered why the ache lingers—even when life looks "better"—it's because grief has its own clock. And it deserves to be felt, honored, and held with compassion.

You are not weak because you still feel it. You are human.

Rebuilding Begins in the Smallest Ways

When I was rebuilding my sense of self, it didn't start with some dramatic transformation. It started with lighting a candle. Sitting in stillness. Touching the scar on my knee and whispering, *I see you.* Wearing the colors I loved. Cooking rice the way my grandmother used to. Allowing tears to come without apology.

It started with letting love back in. Not romantic love—but self-love. Community love. The kind of love that doesn't ask you to fix yourself first. The kind that says: *You're enough even here.*

You do not have to feel whole to start living like you deserve peace. You start by acting like you matter—even when the inner voice doubts it.

That's the healing.

Letting Go of Perfection

One of the hardest lessons for me was learning that healing doesn't mean being perfect.

There were times I'd feel okay—joyful even—and then suddenly a wave of sadness would return. I'd judge myself. *I should be past this. I should know better. I've already done this work.*

But healing isn't linear. It's a spiral. A dance. A rise and fall. And the fall is not failure—it's a returning.

You don't un-become the healed version of yourself just because old pain shows up. You are not starting over—you are deepening.

That realization gave me so much freedom.

Now, when the ache returns, I greet it with tenderness. I say: *I see you. Come sit with me. Let's rest.*

And it always passes. It always softens. Because when we stop resisting the pain, we stop giving it power.

Becoming Your Own Safe Place

Eventually, the most beautiful part of healing is this: you become your own safe place.

Not because nothing hurts anymore, but because you know how to hold yourself in the hurt. You become the one who whispers, *We've survived worse. We'll get through this too.*

You become the one who stays. The one who doesn't abandon yourself, even when the rest of the world feels far away.

That, to me, is the definition of wholeness. Not perfection. Not having it all figured out. But knowing that you belong to yourself—and that is enough.

You Are Not Alone

If you are reading this and your heart feels tender—please know you are not alone.

I am writing these words not from a pedestal, but from the same path. I, too, am rebuilding. I, too, still cry at night sometimes. I, too, have dreams that I continue to do the internal work of believe and trusting in those dreams.

But I also laugh deeply. Love fully. Rest intentionally.
And that is healing.

Let us not rush our becoming.
Let us trust that every time we choose gentleness over shame, presence over panic, and compassion over perfection—
we are rebuilding.
Let us remember that no matter how many pieces you're holding, they all belong to something whole.

You.
Your wholeness was never lost.
It has always lived within you, waiting for your own embrace.

Tools for the Journey:
Restore the Pieces That Still Belong to You

Wholeness is not something we chase—it is something we return to. Not the version of ourselves before the pain, but the deeper truth that survived it. The part of you that knows how to keep breathing when everything else breaks. The part that still dares to hope, even quietly.

There is no one way to come home to yourself. No formula that fits every wound, every loss, every fracture of belonging. But there are tender ways to begin again—through presence, through softness, through love that meets you where you are.

These tools are not instructions. They are invitations. Whether you are rebuilding after trauma, loss, heartbreak, or years of invisibility, may they remind you: healing is not a destination. It is a sacred remembering that you are already whole, even while becoming.

Start by Listening Inward

Wholeness begins not with fixing, but with listening—the kind that doesn't interrupt or rush. Set aside a few minutes each day to check in with yourself, gently and without expectation.

Ask:
– What am I feeling in my body right now?
– What emotion or memory wants to be acknowledged?
– What would help me feel just 1% safer or more grounded today?

Your body holds memory. Your breath carries truth. Even your silence may be asking to be witnessed. Stay with yourself. Even if no words come, let your presence be enough. Listening inward is not passive—it is a radical act of self-trust and the first language of healing.

Release the Urge to "Get Back to Normal"

After rupture, the instinct is to return to what once was. But that "normal" may have cost you rest, joy, or authenticity. It may have been built on survival, not safety.

Instead of asking, *How do I go back?, ask: Who am I now that I know more?*

You do not need to rebuild your life to match someone else's expectation. You are allowed to begin again in a way that feels like freedom.

Healing doesn't ask you to return. It asks you to rise—intentionally, slowly, and in your own way. You are not behind. You are becoming.

Name the Losses You Carry

Grief that remains unnamed becomes heavy. And sometimes, we do not even realize how much we are holding until we speak it.

Try writing down what you've lost—not just people, but pieces of safety, belonging, freedom, or identity. The parts of you that were overlooked, rejected, or misunderstood. Then, beside each one, write: *And I survived.*

This is not to minimize your pain. It is to honour it. To say: *This mattered. And so do I.* Naming what you grieve doesn't make you fragile. It makes you free.

Embrace the Practice of Self-Parenting

When care was inconsistent or conditional, survival taught you not to need. But part of healing is re-learning how to receive what you once lived without.

Self-parenting is the gentle act of becoming your own safe place. It may look like wrapping yourself in warmth when grief visits.

Whispering, *You are safe now* before sleep. Feeding your body with kindness. Laughing for no reason. Taking a nap when the world feels too loud.

This is not indulgence. It is sacred re-parenting. You are not too old to be nurtured. You are right on time. And most of all—you are someone worth staying with.

Redefine Wholeness as Integration, Not Perfection

Wholeness is not the absence of pain. It is the sacred integration of every part of you—the one who fought, the one who froze, the one who ran, and the one who stayed.

Write a letter to the girl you once were. Tell her: *You were brave. You did your best. I see you. I will never leave you behind again.*

You are not healing to become flawless. You are healing to become whole. Not by forgetting your story, but by holding it with love.

Use Gentle Anchors of Routine

When trauma fractures time, rhythm becomes medicine. Choose simple rituals that ground you—not for performance, but for peace.

Light a candle at dusk. Place your hand on your heart each morning and whisper: *I'm still here.* Sip your tea slowly. Let a familiar song hold your breath for a while. Journal your worries without editing them. These are not tasks. They are soul-anchors.

Anchors help your nervous system remember: *You are safe now.* Even in the smallest moments, your presence is a lifeline.

Let Your Dreams Breathe Again

Pain teaches us to be cautious with hope. But your dreams are not gone—they are waiting to be invited back in.

Try this:
– Say one longing out loud, even if your voice shakes
– Write down what joy might feel like in your future
– Imagine thriving—not because you earned it, but because you are worthy of it

Dreaming is not a betrayal of your past. It is a reclamation of your light. You don't have to chase your dreams. You just have to let them exhale again.

Surround Yourself with Safe Presence

Healing doesn't require a crowd—but it does crave witness. Surround yourself with those who see you without asking you to perform. Who honour your process, not just your progress.

This might be a trauma-informed therapist, a soul-friend, a mentor, or even a book that speaks your language when no one else can. It might also be your own reflection saying, *I will not abandon you.*

You only need a few safe souls—and that includes you. Start by speaking to yourself as someone worth staying for.

A Closing Whisper

There will be days when the grief still rises like a wave. When your reflection feels unfamiliar. When joy feels distant and progress invisible.

But healing is not measured by how fast you forget the pain. It is measured by how bravely you keep choosing love—especially toward yourself.

Each time you soften instead of striving, each time you breathe instead of push, you are rebuilding. Not the version of you that once fit the world's mold. But the version that remembers:

I am still here.
I am worthy of care.
I am whole, even in the becoming.

You are not broken. You are becoming.

And that, beloved one, is the quiet revolution of a life rebuilt in love.

CHAPTER 15

To the Girl Who Looks in the Mirror and Sees Only Flaws —

Your reflection is not your rejection.

I know what it feels like to stand in front of a mirror and feel like you are not enough. To stare at your face, your skin, your body—and wonder why it doesn't feel like home. To trace the features someone else labeled as "too much" or "not enough." The curve of your hips. The shade of your skin. The shape of your nose. The softness in your belly. The marks that time or struggle left behind—each one carrying a story that the world taught you to resent.

But I want you to pause for a moment and remember this: you were never meant to be at war with yourself.

Your body is not your enemy. It is your witness. It has carried you through storms, held your breath when words failed you, protected your dreams when you were too tired to speak them aloud. It has kept going—quietly, faithfully—even when you wanted to give up.

And those "flaws"? They are not rejections. They are reminders. Reminders that you are real. That you are here. That you have lived and survived and softened and endured. They are not signs of failure. They are evidence of your humanity.

You do not need to shrink to be lovable. You do not need to edit yourself to be worthy. You are allowed to take up space—in your skin, in your voice, in your presence, in this world.

Somewhere along the way, you were taught to look at yourself through someone else's lens. Maybe it came from a magazine. A classmate. A family member. A passing comment that landed like a wound. You were told to be thinner. Smoother. Quieter. Lighter. Smaller.

But you are not a project to fix. You are not a problem to solve. You are not a mistake to erase or a flaw to hide. You are a soul learning to return home to herself—with tenderness, with truth, and with time.

Healing your reflection does not mean waking up and loving every inch of your body all at once. It means softening the way you speak to yourself. It means whispering, *"I'm trying,"* instead of *"I'm failing."* It means choosing to meet the girl inside the mirror not with judgment—but with care. With curiosity. With compassion.

So today—even if it feels hard—try to look at yourself with kinder eyes. Not to perform love, but to practice it. Try to notice one thing that feels like truth. Like strength. Like softness. Like possibility.

Say thank you to the feet that keep walking. The arms that keep holding. The eyes that have seen so much. The face that has carried joy and sorrow with equal grace.

You are not your flaws. You are not the distorted reflection shaped by someone else's insecurities. You are not a rejection.

You are a radiant, rising, powerful work of art in motion. And your beauty was never meant to be measured. Only remembered.

With all my heart,
Someone who sees you clearly

Life Lesson:
Your Reflection Is Not Your Rejection

Some of us learned to look in the mirror and brace ourselves.
Not for beauty.
Not for love.
But for the harshness of our own thoughts.
For the critiques that arrived before we even had language for them.
For the voice that whispered, *You are too much here... not enough there.*

Maybe it started early. Maybe someone told you your body was wrong. Maybe you noticed how the beautiful girls were praised for being smaller, lighter, quieter. Maybe your reflection started to feel more like a courtroom than a sanctuary. Maybe you were never taught to love what you saw—only to improve it, shrink it, erase it, adjust it.

This chapter is for the girl who still flinches when she sees her own face. The one who gets dressed in the dark. The one who scrolls and compares. The one who has practiced invisibility so long, she forgot what her own softness looks like.

I know her, because I was her.

The First Mirror I Feared

I remember standing in front of the mirror at eleven years old. My family had just arrived in a new country after fleeing war. Everything was unfamiliar. My body was changing, everything was shifting, and I was grieving a life that no longer existed.

And in the mirror, I didn't recognize myself.

Not just because I was in a new land, but because I was carrying the weight of trauma, culture shock, and survival. My skin, my hair, my accent, my clothes—none of it fit the definition of beauty I saw around me. I didn't want to be different; I wanted to disappear.

So I learned to self-correct. To contort my expression into what would be acceptable. To hide behind good grades, behind kindness, behind silence. I stopped asking for space and started performing for it. Because when you believe your reflection is a problem, you spend your life trying to apologize for your presence.

What I didn't know then was that I was never the problem.
The problem was the lens.

How the World Teaches Girls to Disappear

All around us, we are told we must earn our worthiness.

Be prettier. Be quieter. Be smaller. Be more productive. Be less emotional. Be what they want.

Even the well-meaning voices sometimes carry harm:
"You'd be so beautiful if you just..."
"Have you tried losing a little weight?"
"You're brave for wearing that."

And so we internalize the message that our bodies are projects. Our faces are puzzles. Our identities must be proven worthy of love. And when we fail to meet these impossible standards, we blame ourselves.

But here is the truth:
You were never supposed to measure your beauty by their broken scales.

The Mirror Is Not the Authority—You Are

There came a moment in my life—after years of activism, humanitarian work, wearing crowns on pageant stages, and holding hands with girls across refugee camps—when I realized: I had spent so long fighting for others to feel beautiful and worthy, but I still struggled to see that in myself.

I knew how to empower others. But I hadn't fully claimed that same freedom in my own heart.

It was only when I began to meet my reflection with curiosity instead of critique that everything changed. Not overnight. Not in a single affirmation. But gradually, in brave and quiet ways.

I started naming the parts of me I had once rejected. I whispered to my scars: *You are the evidence that I survived.* I traced my stretch marks and said: *You are proof of life.* I looked into my own eyes and whispered: *You are not a problem to fix. You are a home I am learning to return to.*

That's the shift. From shame to sanctuary.

The Wounds That Hide in the Reflection

It is important to know that body image isn't just about vanity. It's often about deeper wounds—about belonging, worthiness, and identity.

Sometimes the way we talk to ourselves in the mirror reflects the pain we haven't named yet.
A girl who feels unloved might blame her body.
A girl who feels unseen might punish herself in silence.
A girl who has never felt safe might seek control through self-critique.

So if this is your story, I want you to know: there is nothing wrong with you for feeling this way.

You are not broken. You are responding to messages the world has handed you for years.

And now, you get to choose a new story.

Learning to See Again

Healing your relationship with your reflection is not a one-time event. It is a lifelong invitation to return to yourself—with tenderness.

You begin by noticing the voice in your head. Is it yours? Or is it someone else's? A teacher's? A parent's? A stranger's comment on social media?

Then, you begin replacing that voice with your own.
One that says:
You are allowed to take up space.
You are allowed to have dreams that don't shrink for others.
You are allowed to be seen—not for who they want you to be, but for who you truly are.

This is how we reclaim the mirror.
By refusing to let it become a weapon.
By reclaiming it as a witness.

Sacred Reflection: Returning to the Child Within

When I was younger, I remember brushing my hair in the tent we lived in after becoming refugees. The mirror I used was cracked, and it rested on a dusty table. Still, I remember loving that quiet moment with myself.

I had nothing—no toys, no proper school, no home—but I had myself.

And for a brief second, I didn't see what was missing. I saw what had survived.

That's the reflection I return to now.
The one that remembers my resilience.
The one that says: *You are still here. And that is beautiful.*

We Are All More Than What the Mirror Shows

Our bodies change.
Our skin weathers storms.
Our eyes hold generations of hope and heartache.

We are not meant to stay frozen in time or fit into one definition.
We are meant to live. To expand. To overflow.

And when the mirror fails to honor that, it is not you who needs to change.
It is the mirror that needs to be reimagined.

Let us redefine beauty by presence. By kindness. By truth.
Let us honor the body that carried us through.
Let us rise each day not to perform, but to be.

A Final Whisper to Your Reflection

If you stood in front of the mirror today and felt the sting of shame...
If you avoided your own eyes...
If you criticized yourself for not being more like "them"...

Take a breath. Place your hand on your heart. And remember:
You are not the sum of someone else's opinions.
You are not the girl who must shrink to be seen.
You are not the flaw. You are the full story.
And the story isn't over.

You are not strange. You are sacred.
You are not flawed. You are a flame.
You are not invisible. You are a vision waiting to be reclaimed.

Tools for the Journey:
Come Home to Your Own Reflection

Healing your relationship with your reflection is not about finally achieving a version of yourself that the world deems "acceptable." It is about remembering that you were never meant to earn your worth through your appearance. Your beauty has always been your aliveness—your breath, your heartbeat, your story.

Here are some tools that may gently support you in rewriting the story you have been told about your body, your face, your presence, and your worth.

Reclaim the Mirror as a Place of Compassion, Not Critique

What if the mirror became a place of reunion—not a battleground? Begin by simply noticing what your inner voice says when you look at yourself. Whose voice is it? Where did you learn to speak to yourself that way? Now soften it. Even if it feels awkward or untrue at first, speak with kindness. It doesn't have to be overly positive or performative—just honest and gentle. Say: "You are still here. That's enough." Or, "I see you." Or, "You are worthy of being loved in this body." You don't have to believe it all at once. You're not performing confidence—you're practicing connection. And that's what healing is: consistent, loving return.

Write a Love Letter to the Body That Carried You Through

Find a quiet moment and write to your body as if it were a loyal friend. Begin with, "Dear body, I haven't always treated you kindly. I'm sorry. I now see you've carried me through…" Then list them: the tears no one saw, the fears you faced quietly, the mornings you rose without strength, the steps you took when the world felt heavy. As you give voice to your body's memory, you begin to move from shame to gratitude—not because your body is perfect, but because it has always been there for you, even when you weren't always there for it.

Shift Your Focus from Appearance to Aliveness

It is easy to get lost in the surface—the reflection, the filters, the comparisons. But healing happens when you shift your gaze from how you look to how you feel. Ask yourself: What makes me feel alive in my body? When do I feel most connected to myself? What movement feels joyful—not punishing? Maybe it's dancing barefoot in your kitchen. Maybe it's resting in a way that says, "I deserve peace." The goal is not to change your appearance. The goal is to return to the truth beneath the gaze of judgment.

Speak to the Younger You in the Mirror

Most of our insecurities began in childhood—before we had the tools to challenge them. If you struggle with self-criticism, try this: look at your reflection and imagine your younger self standing beside you. Maybe she's five. Or ten. Or thirteen. Speak to her gently. Would you tell her she's not good enough? Or would you say, "You are magical just as you are. You don't have to change to be loved. You are allowed to take up space." Often, the healing we long for as adults begins when we return to the child within us and remind her she is already worthy.

Cleanse Your Spaces of Silent Harm

Sometimes, the harm to our self-image isn't loud—it is subtle and constant. It is the stack of beauty magazines. The influencer you follow who never seems real. The friend or family member who always comments on your appearance. Healing requires boundaries. Unfollow accounts that make you feel "less than." Shift conversations away from appearance. Choose to surround yourself with voices that reflect truth, softness, and joy in all expressions of beauty. The way you curate your outer world deeply affects your inner one. Be intentional. You deserve to feel safe in your own presence.

Reframe the Concept of Beauty

What if beauty wasn't a look—but a way of being? What if beauty was presence? Stillness? Laughter lines and softness? A face that reflects truth, not perfection? A body that breathes, endures, stretches, and dances? When you expand your definition of beauty to include your full humanity, you make room for yourself. You don't have to fit into anyone else's frame. You get to define your own—and that, in itself, is beautiful.

Practice Mirrorless Days

This might feel counterintuitive—but some healing begins with a break. If the mirror has become a source of stress or shame, try taking a day—or several—where you don't look in it at all. Let your sense of worth be rooted in your breath, your actions, your relationships—not your reflection. Let yourself feel your life from the inside out. When you return to the mirror, do so with intention—not judgment.

Let Others Reflect Your Light, But Never Define It

Sometimes, healing means letting others reflect what we can't yet see in ourselves. Let friends remind you of your radiance. Let mentors see the light in you when your own vision is clouded. Let kind words be received. But always remember: their words are a mirror, not a measure. Your light is not dependent on praise—it is inherent. Their affirmation may support your healing, but your worth has never been theirs to define.

Choose Ritual Over Routine

Create gentle rituals that reconnect you to your body with tenderness. Light a candle when getting ready. Apply lotion slowly and say, "I am worthy of care." Wear something that feels soft and comforting. Smile at yourself in the mirror the way you would smile at someone you love. These practices may seem small—but they are sacred. They are daily reminders that your body is not a burden. It is your home.

Remember: Wholeness Was Never About Perfection

You don't need to wait until you've "fixed" yourself to begin loving who you are. You don't need to achieve a certain shape or standard to feel beautiful. You don't need to become someone else to feel like you matter. You get to begin here. In this body. In this moment. Not because it is flawless—but because it is yours. Not because you've earned it—but because you were always worthy.

Let your reflection be your invitation—not your rejection.
Let it be the doorway to your own return.
Let it remind you: you are not an object to critique, but a soul to be seen.
And you—just as you are—are already a miracle.

From One Heart to Another —
Surrender: Trust the Dream   *Letter from a champion*

Dear Young Lisa,

I write to you today as a time traveller, visiting my younger self. We are the same soul on the inside; except you are more innocent, and I have more knowledge and life experience.

Lisa, you don't know this yet, but life's biggest journey that you will embark upon is the journey back to yourself—to know who you are, what you stand for, and what you are called to do. Oh, the life lessons you will learn through this journey of self-discovery... even at the age of 54, I am still gaining new insights and a-ha moments every day.

Life has not always been easy, despite appearances to the contrary— maybe start rocking the boat a little more when you are not "feeling it." A big lesson I've learned is don't turn yourself inside out to get others to understand your situation ... that is, don't waste energy trying to convince others of your pain and suffering, as those who don't have your lived experience won't be able to imagine what you're feeling inside—and quite frankly some just won't care. There will be others who care about you for who you are, so surround yourself with people who have a good heart.

Bottom line: when it comes to defining yourself, rather than trying to convince others to see life through your lens, put your energy into learning to self-advocate and to communicate your needs with grace and confidence, just as you've always done when you've stood up for others since you were a tot. You will eventually learn to validate yourself and find your voice, all on your own. Only then will people truly listen to you.

Life's ups and downs often lead to a bumpy road. Sometimes we feel on top of the world, and other times we feel like we are down in the dumps. Grief and loss are especially hard. Take heart, your gift is to seek and find Light, even in the dark corners and mostly during the tough times. Your Faith keeps you going, and your most enlightening lesson was to learn to "Let Go and Let God." With humility, you will realize that the plans that you make for yourself are not always the best ones—don't worry, you'll learn to let go of the outcome.

Love yourself, from the inside out, yes, even the way you look. When I look back through pictures, I realize that I've been way too hard on us— we've been our own biggest critic. This is a lesson that I am still learning: to quell the impulse to be hard on myself. We are a "little stubborn," so patience is key… we'll get there eventually if we keep trying.

The good news is that you will eventually learn self-compassion and not be so hard on yourself, and to love yourself at least as much as your family does. Just as you tried to save countless birds, butterflies, and baby rabbits as a child, you will try to save others—you need to learn that you need to save yourself first. We finally learned this lesson the hard way, after three burnouts… And to be honest, those tough times have been your biggest teachers.

You are very creative and capable, and this is what people want to tap into: your energy, your gifts, and your ability to uplift others. Eventually, you'll learn the difference between setting healthy boundaries versus taking on other people's problems. It is easy to give all your energy away to others, and much harder to recuperate it. My regret is that I didn't learn this sooner. Had I known, perhaps I would have made different choices about when to say, "Yes," when to say, "enough is enough," and when to say a flat-out, unapologetic, "No." This is still a work in progress.

Sure, you received more accolades than you can count, and good salaries and awards… but the cost of your health was far too great. I am sad to report that you will eventually get diagnosed with fibromyalgia, chronic pain, and as it stands, there is a possibility of metabolic syndrome and heart issues. I wish I could have gotten to you sooner. Again, coming back to the need to set boundaries—hopefully, the message will come through loud and clear.

There is also more good news and many things to be grateful for. Life is definitely worth living. Our world and the people and all living things in it—for the most part—are beautiful. When things seem bleak, remember that the sun will rise every day and that sometimes all you need to do to heal is talk to a child, step out onto the grass, and listen to a bird sing.

Thankfully, you will make the best decision when you choose your husband and your lifelong best friend. You will have a beautiful son who will grow into a kind, brilliant, and handsome man (just breathe through the teen years; you've got this). You are fortunate to have had the parents, siblings, and extended family you do, and you have many friends who are beautiful souls. Love is central in our lives and there is plenty for us to share with others, even with people on the other side of the globe.

You will continue to care very deeply for the wellbeing of others, and your calling will be to find all kinds of ways and learn the skills to help the masses, be it through coaching, writing books, delivering talks (oh yes, you will eventually conquer stage fright!), giving hugs, fundraising—one of the most important things you will do is to lift people and their voices, especially the voices of great leaders and the voices of the most vulnerable. It is their stories about dreaming big that will change the world.

So, in closing, don't work so hard, set boundaries, continue to love as much as possible with an open heart and open mind—you are way more powerful than you think. The rest, I will leave it up to you to experience and figure out. You've got this.

Lots of love and gratitude,

Your friend, Lisa Anna Palmer

P.S. Two things: 1) Maybe skip the Parapsychology elective in college and take more accounting instead, and 2) Never stop exercising and keep doing cartwheels (it's really hard to restart from scratch)

P.P.S. There is more to menopause than hot flashes—get informed!

PART VI

Surrender: Trust the Dream

Even when no one else sees it—hold on.

There comes a moment—quiet, unannounced—when the journey shifts. The striving softens. The urgency fades. And suddenly, the path becomes less about proving and more about trusting. Less about running, more about listening. You stand at the edge of becoming, holding a dream so intimate, so sacred, it feels almost too fragile to name aloud.

This part of the journey is not about performance. It is about permission. Permission to believe in something not yet seen. To protect what is still growing. To honour the unfolding—not with force, but with faith.

Surrender, in its truest sense, is not giving up. It is giving in—to the current of your own life. It is trusting the quiet wisdom within you. The dream that stirs at dawn. The knowing that whispers in the stillness. The ache that says: this matters, even if no one else sees it.

To surrender is to stop chasing what the world rewards and start choosing what your soul remembers. It is the sacred shift from "What should I do?" to "What feels true?" From chasing applause to following alignment. From timelines to trust.

This part is for the girl who's building something no one else can yet see. The one who wakes with fire in her chest and doubt in her mind. The one who keeps showing up—without validation, without clarity, without certainty—because something inside her says: keep going.

Here, we learn to co-create with life itself. To hold the vision without forcing the outcome. To rest in divine timing, even when everything feels slow. To believe that the unseen can still become real—especially when it is born from truth.

Your dream is not random. It is not foolish. It is not too late.

It was planted in you for a reason.

And just because others cannot see it, does not mean it is not real.

You are not behind. You are blooming.
Quietly. Powerfully. On time.

So we enter this chapter with open hands and brave hearts.

We listen.
We let go.
We trust.

Not because we know the map—but because we have learned to follow the light within.

This is the surrender.
This is where the dream begins to live.

From One Heart to Another —
Your Path Knows You   *Letter from a champion*

Dearest You,

There's so much I want to say to you—so many truths I've carried through the years that I wish you could hold onto now, especially on the days when you can't tell whether you're in the deepest valley or the highest mountaintop—or the days when you exist in both spaces at the same time. But what I need you to hold onto and inscribe deeply on your heart and spirit are these truths:

Rejection refines me. Redirection realigns me.
Purpose propels me.

This is really important because you will face a lot of rejection. Honestly, you will experience more no's than you can count. But rejection won't define your path. Instead, it will serve as a turning point. Those roads that seem to be dead ends are Divine reroutes, pointing you down the path toward your destiny—not your end, but the beginning of something greater.

Right now, it might feel like every no you hear chips away at your spirit, leaving you feeling like you must prove yourself at every turn. I know—it stings. It really does. Those feelings are real, and rejection hurts, especially when you've poured your heart into something or someone only to be turned away or passed over. It can leave you questioning your value, your place, and your calling. But hear me, you powerful force: "No" is not the end of your story. It is the invitation to turn the page.

What you will discover is that the closed doors, the unanswered calls, the heavy silences—none of them can stop what has been placed inside you. In fact, they will awaken a part of you that refuses to give up, that dares to hope, and that dreams wildly in the face of disappointment. Because you...

You, my girl, are resilient. You will try, do, fail, learn, and do again. And again. And again.

You'll become the kind of person who's not afraid to begin, even when the outcome is uncertain. You'll know that failure doesn't mean you're not worthy. It means you're in motion. It means you're growing.

And you'll grow into something incredible.

Your curiosity will carry you. You will remember that your dad said, "You can do anything as long as you figure out how it works." That will drive you to want to know how things work, why they matter, and how they might be made better—not just for yourself, but for others, too. That hunger to understand, to investigate, to explore won't go away. Feed it. Let it lead you. It will become one of your greatest strengths.

You will not be content with getting by; you will be driven to transform.

You will ask hard questions. You will disrupt what needs disrupting. And when life offers you no after no, you won't shrink. You'll start looking for new ways to get to yes. You'll study the systems, the rules, the patterns. You'll get smart. Strategic. You'll be tough—and yet, you'll remain tender, just like the Father.

That tenderness—that's another power you'll carry. Because the truth is, you'll go through things that feel too heavy for someone your age. You'll be hurt. You'll be broken in places that might take years to mend. But none of it will define you. None of it will keep you down. In fact, those wounds will deepen your compassion and help you lead with love, care, and dignity. You will remember what it felt like to be underestimated, dismissed, and abandoned. And you will become someone who does what you can so others don't experience that same pain. You will walk with people in their grief and their joy, without needing them to hurry to the other side. You will listen deeply. You will see clearly. And because of this, people will trust you. They will follow you. And together, you will build something that matters.

Even when you feel small—even when you doubt yourself—there is a fire in you that won't go out. That fire is your vision.

You'll see possibilities others don't. You'll ask, "What if?" when others say, "It's always been this way." You'll imagine what the world could be like if it were a little softer, a little fairer, a little more beautiful—and you won't just imagine it. You'll work for it.

When others say, "It can't be done," I want you to say, "Yes, let's."

When others tell you to play it safe, I want you to ask, "But what if we're meant for bigger and better?"

When fear whispers, "What if you fail?" I want you to answer, "Then I'll try again."

Because you will fail. And that's okay—because you will win so much more.

You'll try things that don't work. You'll pour yourself into people and projects that fall apart. You'll lose opportunities. You'll get knocked down. But none of that will stop you. You'll keep moving. You'll keep rising.

Every time you fall, you'll learn. And every time you learn, you'll do better. That's how you'll grow into someone who leads, builds, heals, and transforms.

You will be innovative. You'll make something out of nothing. You'll create pathways where others only saw dead ends. You'll lead with your heart and your head, using knowledge and wisdom like twin flames. You'll take the rejection and use it as fuel to prove them wrong—and prove to yourself that you can. You'll use what you've gained to unlock something new for yourself, and more importantly to you, for others. Because your gifts aren't just for you.

Your curiosity, courage, care, and commitment will ripple outward. They will strengthen your family. They will light up your community. They will influence your city. They will impact your country. And yes—they will touch the world.

*So don't be afraid of dreaming big. Actually, dream **BIGGER.** Because if God gives exceedingly and abundantly more than you can ask, think, or imagine, that means if you can conjure it up, He can (and will!) give you bigger and better. The dreams that feel wild and impossible right now—some will come true. Others will evolve into things even more beautiful than you imagined. And some will fade. What will shape you, though, is that even those faded dreams will leave behind wisdom that forms your next chapter. You carry them all, and they all work together for your good.*

Remember this:

God has given you the world—not to carry, but to explore, love, and help move forward.

You won't do it perfectly. I promise, you'll mess up. But you'll never stop doing the good work of doing good work—leaving the world better than you found it.

So here's my invitation to you:

Say yes to goodness—even when it's scary, uncomfortable, or the outcome is unknown.
Say yes to learning. To failing and rising again—because when you know better, you do better.
Say yes to dreaming big and loving bigger.
Say yes to your voice, your vision, your worth—because you are so worth it.
Say yes to hope. To the simple belief in what could be when a good God has willing hands.
Say yes, let's—again and again.

One day, you'll look back at all the rejection and all the failure, and you'll see that in the end, you may have lost some—but you've won so much more… exceedingly and abundantly more.

Keep going, beautiful girl.
Try. Fail. Learn. Do.
Do again.
And win.

All my love,
Your future self,

Austen

CHAPTER 16

To the Girl Who Wants to Lead —

Your Voice Is Your Vision

Not every leader begins with a stage.
Some begin with a quiet conviction. A stirring in the chest.
A whisper that says, *This matters.*

You may not wear a title yet.
You may not have a seat at every table.
You may still hesitate when you speak.
But that does not mean you are not a leader.

Leadership often begins in unseen places—with a choice, a value,
a question no one else is brave enough to ask out loud.

Your voice—your way of seeing the world, of noticing what is
missing, of caring deeply, of daring to imagine something better—
is already shaping change.

Leadership isn't always loud.
It doesn't always come with applause.
Sometimes, it looks like showing up when it's hard.
Sometimes, it's being the first to speak when silence is safest.
Sometimes, it's daring to be kind in a room full of noise.

If you've ever looked around and thought, *There has to be a better
way*—that, right there, is your vision.

If you've ever held space for someone when no one else would—that is leadership.

If you've ever felt the urge to change something, to challenge injustice, to build belonging—that is the beginning of power.

You do not need permission to lead.
You do not need to wait for a title, an invitation, or a perfect version of yourself to arrive.

The world doesn't need more performance. It needs presence.

It needs leaders who lead from truth, not ego. From empathy, not fear. From the quiet strength it takes to remain soft in a world that rewards hardness.

So speak—not to impress, but to stand in alignment with your values.
Dream—not for applause, but because your vision is sacred.
Act—not to prove you are worthy, but because you already are.

The future is not waiting to be handed to you.
It is waiting to be shaped—by your fire, your clarity, your grace.

You are not "too young," "too sensitive," "too late," or "too much."
You are right on time.

Leadership doesn't mean having all the answers.
It means having the courage to begin.

Your voice is not just for speaking.
It is for vision.
And the world is waiting for what only you can lead.

With fierce belief,
Someone who sees the leader in you.

Life Lesson:
Your Voice Is Your Vision

Leadership doesn't always begin with a title, a podium, or a plan. Sometimes, it begins with a whisper—an instinct so quiet it almost goes unnoticed, but powerful enough to shift the course of a life.

I still remember my first whisper.

I was eight years old, sitting in my communion class, when the teacher asked, "Who wants to lead the choir for communion Sunday?" My hand shot up before I had time to second-guess it. I didn't ask my parents. I didn't rehearse it in my head. I just said yes.

That Sunday, in front of a packed church, I stood tall—small in size, but full of purpose—guiding voices into harmony. My parents watched in shock. But for me, something had quietly awakened: I could lead.

It wasn't because I was the best singer. It was because I trusted the voice within me that said, "This is yours to do."

That voice stayed with me, even when war forced my family to flee. From church pews to refugee camps, leadership shifted forms—from choir songs to survival. I no longer led with music. I led by caring for younger siblings, calming chaos with stories, translating adult fears into hope for children. I led with presence, not position.

Even then, a quiet voice beneath the fear whispered, *You are meant for more.*

For a long time, I believed leadership belonged to those who spoke the loudest, moved with certainty, and never questioned their place. I watched others command rooms, and I doubted whether I had what it took.

What I didn't realize was that I wasn't missing the skill to lead—I was missing the permission to believe that I could.

No one tells young girls that leadership often begins in quiet places. That it can look like being the only one who notices something is wrong. That it can rise not from control, but from compassion. That our voices—whether trembling or steady—are already vessels for vision.

Leadership Is Not Something You Become.
It's Something You Remember.

Leadership is not a role we grow into. It's a truth we return to.

When I arrived in a new country and began rebuilding my life, that voice came back again and again. It nudged me to volunteer, to speak up, to enter rooms where no one else looked like me. It reminded me that I belonged—even when the world tried to convince me otherwise.

Some of us are born into spaces that try to shrink our light. But the vision doesn't disappear just because the room is small. The dream doesn't dissolve just because others can't see it.

Leadership is not about having the loudest voice. Sometimes, it's the girl who wakes her siblings early so her parents can rest. Sometimes, it's the teenager who starts a mental health club while managing her own anxiety. Sometimes, it's the woman who chooses to lead from the back, guiding others through grief or growth with nothing but her presence.

Real leadership lives in courage, not noise. In vision, not volume. In presence, not perfection.

Let Go of Who the World Told You to Be

To step into true leadership, you must first release the version of yourself the world told you to become.

For years, I believed I had to be more serious, less emotional, more "acceptable" to lead. I tried to polish myself into something people would respect. But I've learned that respect earned through inauthenticity is fragile. What endures is truth.

The world does not need more leaders who dominate. It needs more who listen. Who lift. Who dare to lead from love.

You do not need to shrink to be taken seriously. You do not need to become smaller to become strong.

When the Dream Feels Too Big

I once told someone I wanted to be Miss Canada. They laughed. "Girls like us don't win things like that," they said.

They were wrong.

Years later, I stood on that stage—not just wearing a crown, but honoring every girl who had ever been told her dream was unrealistic. I didn't win because I fit the mold. I won because I shattered it.

Your vision is not too much. It is not an accident. It was planted within you for a reason.

Even if no one claps.
Even if no one sees it.
Even if it feels too early.

Hold on.

Some of the Most Powerful Leadership Moments Are Unseen

I've stood on stages before thousands. And I've also led from the quiet corners—offering tissues to a friend, standing up for a child, choosing compassion when it cost me influence. Both are leadership.

If you've been told leadership only counts when it's public, polished, or praised, I invite you to reclaim your own definition.

You lead every time you choose love over fear.
You lead every time you speak up from your truth.
You lead every time you show up for someone else—
and for yourself.

Before I Could Lead Others, I Had to Learn to Lead Myself

That meant listening to the still, sacred voice within me. The one that knew I was meant to help build the kind of world I didn't get to grow up in.

That voice did not always shout. It often whispered. But every time I honored it—whether through journaling, prayer, or presence—it grew stronger. And eventually, it became a compass.

When you stop asking, "Who will let me?" and start asking, "What do I know to be true?"—you begin to lead with clarity, not fear.

A Different Kind of Leadership

Some of the most powerful leaders are not found in headlines. They are found in hallways, homes, and hospital rooms. They lead with tears in their eyes and fire in their bones. They lead not to be seen, but to serve.

You don't need a crown. You need a mirror.

Because true leadership isn't about elevating yourself—it's about elevating others. When you lead with your heart, you become a reflection. A permission slip. A spark.

Your Voice Is Not Too Soft

It is a quiet kind of strength.
It carries wisdom generations long.
It is not for everyone to understand—but it is yours to use.

Leadership is not about being the first.
It's about being the truest.
And the world needs your truth more than ever.

So say yes—even if your voice shakes.
Say yes—even if the path is not clear.
Say yes—even when you're scared.

Because every yes you give to your purpose is a no to the silence that once kept you small.

And one day, a girl will watch you lead and whisper, "If she can, so can I."

That's how the legacy begins.

Your voice is your vision.

Let it rise.

Tools for the Journey:
Become the Leader You Already Are

Leadership does not begin with certainty. It begins with awareness—the kind that listens before it speaks, sees before it reacts, and cares before it controls. The call to lead often arrives quietly. Not as a title. Not with fanfare. But as a stirring. A quiet knowing that something must change—and that perhaps, you are the one meant to begin.

This is not about waiting until you feel ready. It is about recognizing the leader already living inside you. Even in your most tender, unfinished places. Especially there. These tools are not about performance. They are about presence. About rooting into who you are—so you can rise into who you are becoming.

Reclaim the First Time You Felt Like a Leader

Think back. Not to a title or a stage—but to a moment when you acted from truth, even if your voice trembled. Maybe it was when you spoke up for someone who had been silenced. Maybe it was when you held your family together in the middle of chaos. Or when you made a brave decision rooted in love instead of fear.

It may not have been called leadership then. But it was. That moment counts. Write the story down. Name it for what it truly was. Let it remind you that you have led before, even without a map, even without applause. And you will lead again.

Listen for the Inner Voice

In a world full of noise, clarity becomes a sacred act of resistance. Each day, gift yourself a few minutes of stillness. No title to wear. No problem to solve. No one to impress. Just breath, awareness, and your own unfolding.

Ask yourself gently:

What is rising in me today?
What truth am I afraid to say aloud?
What would love do next?

You may not hear an answer right away, but the asking matters. Your inner knowing is soft, but it is ancient. Trust it. It is not there to impress the world—it is there to guide you home.

Stop Waiting for Permission

Leadership is not something you wait to be given. It is something you choose. You do not need a crown to care. You do not need credentials to make a difference. You do not need someone else to tell you you're ready before you begin.

Start where you are—with what breaks your heart, with what keeps you up at night, with what lights a fire in your spirit. The moment you choose yourself—the moment you say, "Yes, I will"—the world begins to rearrange itself around that decision. That is the beginning of leadership.

Redefine What a Leader Looks Like

You do not have to be loud to be powerful. You do not have to be fearless to be brave. You do not have to be perfect to lead. You are allowed to cry and still be strong. You are allowed to lead from softness and still be bold.

Let go of the leadership models rooted in control, burnout, or performance. You get to build a leadership shaped by presence, empathy, courage, and deep care. This is not a role you play. It is not a crown you wear. It is a life you live—with love and intention at the center.

Know the Difference Between Noise and Wisdom

Not every voice that reaches you deserves your attention. Not every opinion needs a seat at the table of your becoming. When someone questions your dream, pause. Ask yourself: *Is this fear speaking or love? Is this rooted in truth or insecurity?*

Discernment is not dismissal—it is protection. You are allowed to walk away from voices that confuse your calling. Trust your inner wisdom to separate the static from the sacred.

Embrace the Power of Not Knowing

You do not need to see the entire path to begin. The greatest leaders often started in uncertainty, guided not by certainty but by conviction. Let curiosity lead you when clarity hasn't arrived yet. Let courage carry you where certainty cannot go.

Leadership is not about always knowing the answer. It is about showing up anyway—with presence, with humility, and with the willingness to grow. You are not expected to have it all figured out. You are only asked to stay true and keep moving with love.

Build a Circle That Honors Your Becoming

You cannot do this alone—and you were never meant to. Find the ones who see your becoming as sacred. The ones who speak life into your leadership, not because you've arrived, but because you are still becoming.

Surround yourself with people who do not flinch when you are uncertain. Who does not require you to perform your strength. Be in the company of those who hold your growth with reverence. Leadership may begin with you—but it is nurtured in the community. And sustained relationships.

Let Purpose Anchor You

There will be days when everything feels heavy. When progress is invisible and the weight of your role feels unbearable. In those moments, come back to your why.

Return to the story that shaped you. The reason you first said yes. The longing that keeps you rooted in something greater than yourself. You are not doing this only for you. You are lighting a path for someone else to walk through behind you. That is purpose. Let it be your anchor when everything else feels adrift.

Your Voice Is the Vision

Your voice carries more than sound. It carries your history, your hopes, your heartbreak, and your healing. Even if it shakes, even if it has been silenced before, it is still worthy. It is not decoration—it is direction.

Speak not to be seen, but to serve. Lead not to be celebrated, but to create space for others to rise. Your voice doesn't just describe the vision—it is the vision. And the world needs it now—more than ever.

A Final Word for the Becoming Leader

You are already becoming her. Not through perfection. Not through applause. But through every quiet decision to show up, to stay true, to begin again.

This is your leadership. It is not borrowed. It is not assigned. It is born of your becoming—each step, each breath, each choice made with love.

You do not have to wait.
You are already walking in it.

CHAPTER 17

To the Girl Who's Scared to Speak Up —

Courage whispers first

I know what it feels like to have something to say—yet keep it locked inside. To rehearse your truth a hundred times in your mind, only to stay silent when the moment arrives.

You tell yourself it is not the right time. That your words are not ready. That your feelings are too much, your thoughts not polished enough, your voice not steady enough to carry the weight of what matters to you.

But here is what I want you to remember:

Courage does not always roar. It does not always arrive with certainty or applause.

Most often, it begins as a whisper.

A quiet, persistent nudge that says, *Maybe it's time.*

That whisper is not random. It is sacred. It's the sound of your truth trying to reach the surface.

You do not need to have it all figured out. You do not need to speak eloquently. You only need to begin—with honesty, with heart, with the deep knowing that your voice deserves space in the world.

Sometimes, the words feel stuck because they come from tender places—soft spaces inside you that have not always been welcomed or protected. That's okay. Go gently. But do not mistake silence for safety.

Sometimes what feels safe is simply what is familiar. And familiar is not the same as free.

There is a voice within you that remembers who you are. It has waited patiently—through the noise, through the doubt, through the years you spent shrinking so others could feel more comfortable.

Let that voice rise.

Even if your hands tremble.
Even if your voice cracks.
Even if tears come halfway through the sentence.

Courage is not the absence of fear—it is the decision to speak even while afraid.

To say, *I matter. This matters.*
To risk being seen in the fullness of your truth.

Your voice is not a burden. It is a bridge—to healing, to connection, to change.

Use it gently. Use it boldly. But above all, use it.

You are not too quiet to be powerful.
You are not too soft to be heard.
You are not too scared to be brave.

Speak, beloved. The world may not be listening yet—but it needs your whisper.

With love,
Someone who found her voice, one quiet word at a time.

Life Lesson:
Courage Whispers First

I know what it feels like to sit with truth in your heart—to feel a message building inside like gentle rain before a storm—yet remain frozen. To rehearse your words a thousand times in your mind, only to fade into silence the moment someone's eyes meet yours.

You tell yourself, *Not now. Not yet.* That your feelings are too raw, your voice not ready, your thoughts too messy. But what if the moment you're waiting for isn't meant to be perfect? What if it's sacred because your voice belongs there—trembling, unfiltered, and beautifully alive?

Yes, I'm writing this to you—the one whose words are still hidden behind a veil of fear. The one who wonders if her voice even matters. Take a deep breath. You and I—we are in this together. And I need you to know: your voice is more powerful than you realize. Here is why.

Courage Doesn't Roar — It Begins as a Whisper

We often think courage looks like grand gestures and unshakable confidence. But most often, it starts quietly—an inner whisper that says, *Maybe it's time.* It's that soft nudge in your chest that dares you to share, to ask, to name what you've been holding.

I first heard that whisper when I was twelve. New to a school, new to a country, new to everything. I wanted to tell the girls around me that I didn't know how to fit in. That loneliness was sitting heavy in my chest. My throat tightened. My legs shook. But still, I said it: *"I'm scared."* That whisper cracked something open. It invited tenderness. It made room for truth.

That moment taught me that courage doesn't need volume to be brave. It only needs honesty.

Silence Isn't Always Safe

There's a myth that silence is neutral. That if you stay quiet, no one will notice your fears or your doubts. But silence, over time, becomes a cage.

When you hold pain, anger, or truth inside, it starts to shape you. Your voice is meant to move, to stretch, to breathe. To transform tension into clarity, and isolation into connection.

The world cannot change without your truth. Even one small word can spark a ripple that reaches further than you know.

What If Your Voice Is the Change Someone Needs?

There is power in vulnerability. A girl who admits she is struggling makes space for others to do the same. A woman who shares her burnout invites others to rest. A survivor who tells her story unlocks empathy where silence once lived.

Your voice is not only for you. It's a hand extended to someone who thought she was alone. It's a light for someone still searching. When you speak, you give others permission to do the same.

That is leadership.

Why We Stay Silent

So often, silence is not a choice—it's protection. Maybe you were raised to be polite, quiet, agreeable. Maybe you were shamed, ignored, or dismissed when you spoke. Maybe you learned that being small kept you safe.

These were survival strategies. They are not your fault. But they don't have to remain your truth.

Now, you are allowed to choose again.

Begin by noticing when fear silences you. Does your throat tighten? Do your shoulders tense? What voices rise within you? Name them. Meet them not with judgment, but with compassion.

Breath is an Anchor

When fear rises, begin with breath.

Place a hand on your heart. Inhale deeply. Hold for a moment. Exhale slowly.

Let your body remember: you are here. You are safe enough to speak. You are allowed to take up space.

Breathing doesn't erase fear. But it gives it a place to be held—so that courage can rise beside it.

Confidence Is a Slow Becoming

Confidence doesn't arrive in a single moment. It is shaped over time—through whispered truths, small declarations, and honest conversations.

Speak first to yourself. Journal your thoughts. Read them aloud. Then try speaking with a trusted friend, a mentor, or a mirror. Let your voice stumble and still be sacred. Each word you say builds trust in yourself. Each truth you own makes the next one easier.

Boundaries Are Part of Voice, Too

Using your voice doesn't mean exhausting it. You are allowed to rest. You are allowed to say "not right now." You are allowed to pause between brave acts.

Healing doesn't mean you must be fearless every day. It means you know when to speak, when to step back, and when to breathe before rising again.

Find Your Safe Witnesses

You do not need to speak into a void. Begin with those who see you clearly. People who listen with tenderness. Who mirror back your worth. Who create space for your voice to stretch and grow.

Your voice will find its strength more easily when it is first welcomed with care.

Speak—Even If It Shakes

When you speak despite the tremble in your voice, that is courage. When your truth rises through tears, that is authenticity.

Let your voice be imperfect. Let it crack. Let it cry. Let it feel.

Your humanity is not a hindrance. It is your greatest authority.

Your Words Will Create Ripples

Maybe someone won't respond right away. Maybe the room stays quiet. But that does not mean your voice went unheard.

Words have echoes. Your truth may reach someone days later. Your whisper may awaken something in a stranger's heart.

Trust the ripples, even if you don't see them yet.

Trust the Whisper as a Sign

I have spoken quiet truths in places where no one expected them— in refugee camps, classrooms, boardrooms. I have seen soft words change hearts, shift systems, and move people toward justice.

That whisper you feel? It's not just a feeling. It is direction. It is alignment.

Even if the world doesn't hear it loudly, your soul does. And that is enough.

An Invitation: Speak for Healing

Let today be the day you whisper one truth into the world. You could say:

"I'm afraid, but I'm trying."
"I need help."
"That hurt me."
"I want something more."
Or even simply: "I matter."

It doesn't need to be grand. It just needs to be yours.

Let it rise. Let it land. Let it begin to set you free.

In Closing: Courage is a Daily Return

There is no finish line for bravery. It lives in the daily choice to trust your voice again.

When your family questions your path, say: "This dream still matters to me."

When a peer dismisses you, say: "My voice deserves space here."

When you feel small after speaking, remind yourself: "I spoke. I showed up. I am still here."

That is what it means to surrender to your voice—not with loud certainty, but with unwavering presence.

We are all learning to speak, whisper, and lead ourselves forward.

And you, beloved—you are not too late. Not too quiet. Not too much.

You are right on time. Your voice is not just your vision.

It is the first breath of your becoming.

Tools for the Journey:
Find Strength in the Soft Sound of Your Voice

There is a stillness before every act of courage. A breath. A pause. A quiet reckoning with truth.

For some, that pause lasts seconds. For others, it stretches across years. Especially if silence became your shield—if quiet kept you safe, unseen, or simply tolerated.

But courage does not always begin with the roar. Sometimes, it begins with the tremble. With the whisper. With the part of you that's ready, even if the rest is still afraid.

These tools are not about making you louder. They are about helping you become more fully yourself.

Recognize Your Inner Knowing

You do not need the world's permission to know what you know.

Often, what silences us is not confusion—it is doubt. Doubt seeded by a world that conditioned us to question our instincts.

Ask yourself gently:

What truth have I been carrying in secret?

What wisdom keeps rising in me, even when I try to suppress it?

Your voice begins not in what you say to others, but in what you're willing to admit to yourself. Let your truth live there first—quietly, fully, freely.

Practice Safe Expression

You do not have to speak your truth in unsafe places to prove your courage. Start with sanctuary. A journal. A voice note. A letter that never needs to be sent.

Let your voice land somewhere that welcomes it. Let it stretch. Let it breathe.

When you're ready, seek out spaces that hold your truth with tenderness—a trusted friend, a mentor, a room that feels kind.

Bravery begins in safety. Give your voice the soil it needs to grow strong.

Tune In to Your Body's Language

Your voice does not just come from your throat—it lives in your body.

Pay attention.

What happens when you silence yourself? Does your jaw tighten? Your shoulders rise?

And what happens when you finally say what you mean—even if it's just to yourself?

Your body is fluent in honesty. It will show you when you are shrinking and when you are returning.

Let it guide you back to your truth.

Release the Myth That Loud Equals Strong

Your voice does not have to fill a room to matter.

Courage is not always public. Sometimes it whispers a soft "no" when everyone else expects "yes."

Let go of the idea that you must be fierce to be powerful.

Gentleness is power. Thoughtfulness is power.

The world may not always reward your softness—but that does not mean it is not strength.

Build a Trust Contract—with Yourself

If your voice has been dismissed, ignored, or punished, it makes sense that you've learned to second-guess it.

But you can begin again.

Try writing a contract to your future self:

"I will not abandon my truth to make others comfortable."
"I will stay with myself—even when it's hard."
"I will listen to the voice within me before the voices around me."

This is not about being fearless. It is about being faithful—to the girl who still wants to speak.

Give Yourself Time—But Do Not Stay Silent Forever

You are allowed to move at your own pace.

Silence was survival once. You do not need to rush into sound.

But there will come a time when your truth no longer fits inside your silence.

When the ache of holding it in becomes heavier than the fear of letting it out.

When that moment comes—let yourself speak. Even if your voice shakes. Especially then.

Be Okay with Being Misunderstood

Not everyone will understand your voice.

Some people only loved the version of you that stayed quiet. That bent. That disappeared.

Let them go.

Being misunderstood is painful—but not as painful as betraying yourself.

Your truth is not measured by other people's comfort. It is measured by your alignment.

Stay true—even when it costs you approval. Especially then.

Celebrate Your Bravery—Out Loud

Every time you speak, even in the smallest way, honor it.

The message you sent. The truth you whispered. The boundary you named.

These are not small things. They are sacred.

Let your voice speak not only pain, but joy. Wonder. Desire. Dreams.

Say "I want more." Say "I matter." Say "I am here."

Your voice was never only meant to survive. It was meant to sing.

A Closing Whisper for the Brave and Becoming

You do not need to roar to be powerful.

You only need to be honest.

Even if no one claps. Even if your voice trembles. Even if you are the first in your family, your community, your circle to say, "No more."

Trust the whisper.

It will grow.

It always does.

CHAPTER 18

To the Girl With a Story to Tell —

The world needs your truth.

There is a story living inside you—not just one you've lived, but one you've survived. A story shaped by ache and wonder. A story made of quiet moments no one else noticed. A story still unfolding, even now.

Maybe you have carried it in silence for years, unsure if it matters. Maybe you've tried to write it down and stopped halfway, afraid it wasn't enough. Or perhaps you've shared pieces of it, only to feel exposed, misunderstood, or uncertain if it was ever truly safe to be that seen.

But here is the truth: your story was never meant to stay hidden.

The world needs voices like yours—tender, trembling, brave. Voices that do not wait for perfection. Voices that speak from the middle of the journey, not just the end. Voices that remind us we are not alone in the complexity of being human.

Your truth does not have to be polished to be powerful. You do not need to wait until you feel "healed enough" or "whole enough" to begin. Someone out there needs to hear your words exactly as they are—imperfect, honest, alive.

Because when you tell your story, you don't just liberate yourself. You open a window. You light a candle. You give someone else permission to exhale.

Your voice creates a ripple. Your vulnerability carries light. And every time you choose truth over silence, you widen the path for others to walk beside you.

So write the chapter. Speak the memory. Share the scar. Let your truth breathe. Not for applause. Not for validation. Not for anyone else's expectations. But because your story is your soul's way of remembering—and reclaiming—what has always been yours: freedom, voice, belonging.

The world may not be ready. But your soul is. And that's enough.

With quiet courage and deep belief in you,
Someone who knows stories change the world.

Life Lesson:
The Story You Carry Is the Light We Need

There is a quiet moment in nearly every storyteller's journey—the one before the first word is spoken or written. The breath before the truth escapes. That moment is heavy with memory, fear, reverence, and possibility. If you are holding a story you've never told, I want you to know: the silence you've been sitting with is not empty. It is full of becoming.

Telling your story is not just about finding the courage to speak. It is about trusting that your truth is sacred, even when others may not yet understand it. It is about honoring your experiences—even the ones that made you feel small—as worthy of voice, worthy of space, worthy of being held with both dignity and light.

The Silence I Carried

I used to think my story didn't matter. That the world had enough noise and did not need the tremble of my voice added to it. That the things I had endured—the war I survived, the displacement, the loneliness of becoming someone new in a foreign land—were meant to be endured quietly.

But silence has a way of shaping you. It presses against your ribs. It makes your smile tighter and your back straighter. It makes you efficient, composed, and invisible.

Until the day comes when the silence becomes heavier than the truth.

I remember sitting with my journal as a teenager, writing a line that felt like it might break me: *"I still remember the sound of bombs."* I stopped there. My hands trembled. I closed the notebook. Because telling the truth isn't just about the facts—it is about what those facts did to your body, to your breath, to your sense of safety. It is about returning to the moment and choosing to hold your own hand through it.

It took me years to write that line again—and longer to share it with someone else. But the first time I did, I saw something change. In their eyes. In mine. I didn't need to be "fine." I needed to be real. And that realness didn't weaken me. It freed me.

Stories as Seeds of Light

Every one of us has a truth that aches to be shared—not because we want attention, but because we want connection. We want to be understood. We want someone to say: "Me too." Or "I see you now." Or "Thank you for saying that out loud. I needed to hear it."

Your story is not just for you. It is medicine for someone else. It is the light someone else is stumbling toward.

That doesn't mean you owe the world your pain. It means you get to choose—when, how, and with whom you share it. But never doubt that your story is needed.

What If They Don't Believe Me?

This fear is real, especially for those who have been silenced, dismissed, or betrayed. It's not easy to hand over a piece of your soul and pray that it is received with care.

But the truth is not validated by belief. The truth is sacred because it is yours. It stands whether others understand it or not.

If you've ever shared your truth and been met with doubt—please hear this: that reaction is not a reflection of your worth. It is a reflection of their readiness. Some people won't understand your pain because they've never looked at their own. Some won't be able to hold your story because they haven't learned to hold space.

But that doesn't mean you stop telling it. Tell it anyway—softly, boldly, quietly, loudly, in art, in action, in whispers, in declarations. Tell it not for applause, but for alignment. Tell it because every time you do, you return to yourself.

The Truth Does Not Break You—Hiding It Does

I once met a woman who said she had never told anyone that she was abused as a child. She said it with such stillness, such practiced detachment, that it almost felt like a fact about someone else.

And then she said, *"But I feel it in my body every day."*

We carry what we don't name. It lives in our muscles, our breath, our posture, our fears. And healing begins the moment we allow ourselves to say, *"This happened."* Not to re-live it—but to release its grip.

The truth does not break you. Hiding it does.

Shame thrives in secrecy. But when we speak our story—when we own it, not as a wound to be ashamed of but as a truth to be honored—we reclaim our power. We stop apologizing for our scars. We start recognizing them as sacred sites of survival.

Your Truth Will Evolve—Let It

One of the most beautiful parts of telling your story is that it will change over time. Not because it's less true, but because you are healing.

The first time I spoke about being a refugee, I wept. I was still inside the pain. I hadn't yet found the edges of my strength.

Years later, I shared the same story—but from a place of remembrance, not re-wounding. I wasn't speaking to be rescued. I was speaking to remind someone else that they are not alone.

Let your story evolve. Let it breathe. Let it soften and sharpen and shift as you grow. There is no "right" version. There is only the honest one.

You Do Not Need to Be Fully Healed to Speak

One of the most common lies we tell ourselves is: *"I'll share this when I'm over it."* But sometimes, the speaking is part of the healing.

You don't need to be whole to be worthy of voice. You don't need to have all the answers to share what you've learned so far. You don't need to have a perfect arc, or resolution, or takeaway. You just need to be real. And brave. And willing.

The world is aching for authenticity.

You do not need to shout your story from a stage. Maybe your story is shared in a coffee shop. In a letter. In a piece of art. In a moment of stillness when you finally speak it aloud to yourself.

That counts. That heals. That matters.

Storytelling as Sacred Reclamation

To share your truth is to reclaim yourself.

It is to say: *I am no longer hiding to make others comfortable. I am no longer carrying this alone. I am no longer pretending that what happened didn't shape me.*

Because it did. And still, you are here. You are here. And that is something sacred.

You survived what tried to silence you. You lived through what you didn't think you could. You carried truths that the world wasn't ready to hear, and you're still becoming.

That is powerful. That is holy. That is the root of every revolution.

You Are the Author of Your Becoming

No matter what has been written about you—no matter the labels, the gossip, the assumptions, the narratives others tried to assign—you are the author now.

You get to choose the tone. The truth. The timing.

And your story doesn't have to end with trauma. It can move toward triumph. Toward joy. Toward possibility. It can be a love letter to every girl who once thought she had to shrink to survive. It can be a battle cry, a soft song, or a simple whisper.

It can be whatever you need it to be.

But please—don't leave it unsaid.

Not because the world demands it.

But because your soul deserves it.

Tools for the Journey:
Share Your Truth With Tender Power

You do not need a microphone to matter.
You do not need a stage to speak what is sacred.
You do not need perfect words to begin.
You only need your voice—and your willingness to trust it.

Telling your story is not about performance. It is about presence. Whether whispered to the wind or written on tear-stained paper, sharing your truth is a gentle act of reclamation. It says: I lived. I hurt. I healed. I am still becoming. And I am worthy of being witnessed.

But how do you share a truth wrapped in fear or shame? How do you open the door to something so intimate, when the world has not always been kind? These tools are tender companions for that journey—toward your voice, your healing, and your rightful place in the story of this world.

Begin by Listening Inward

Before your story meets the world, let it meet you.

Turn down the volume of comparison, and turn toward the quiet stirrings within. You do not have to start with the hardest chapter. Begin with what feels ready. Maybe it is a moment that keeps tugging at your heart. A memory that surfaces during quiet walks. A phrase you keep writing without realizing. Let that be your invitation.

Stories don't always arrive as full sentences. Sometimes they come as sensations, as images, as small truths that want to be heard. However yours comes, welcome it without judgment.

Feel Before You Share

Some stories need to be felt before they are spoken. Especially the ones born from trauma, violation, or betrayal.

Let yourself feel it fully—without rushing into words. Tears are not weakness. They are thresholds. Breath is not delay. It is a return.

You do not have to prove your strength by sharing before you are ready. And you do not have to prove your worth by staying silent forever. The question is not "Should I share?" but rather, "Does this feel like liberation or re-wounding?"

You are not here to bleed for others' understanding. You are here to heal on your own terms.

Release the Pressure to Perform

Your story is not a speech. It does not need to be polished, poetic, or profound to matter.

We often believe that our truth must inspire others to be valid. But inspiration is not the purpose of your story—integrity is.

Say it awkwardly. Say it with pauses. Say it even if your voice breaks halfway through. Realness reaches further than perfection ever could.

You are not a character. You are the narrator. Tell it like it is—for no one else but you.

Choose Safe, Soul-Honoring Spaces

Your truth deserves to land in spaces that know how to hold it. Not everyone will. That is not a reflection of your worth—it is a reflection of their readiness.

Begin with someone who honors your humanity. A journal. A spiritual elder. A therapist. A sister-friend. A circle that listens without rushing to fix or question.

Some stories do not belong to public platforms. Not yet. Maybe not ever. That doesn't make them less powerful. It makes them sacred.

Rewrite the Meaning, Not the Memory

You may never be able to change what happened. But you can change how it lives inside you.

Many of us were taught to hide the most tender parts of our stories. To tuck away our pain so that others could stay comfortable. But healing begins when we reclaim the narrative.

Try this: Instead of asking "Why did this happen to me?" ask "What wisdom has this story revealed in me?"

This is not erasure. It is transmutation. It is how you stop carrying the story as a wound—and start holding it as a well.

Let Go of Outcome, Cling to Alignment

Sometimes your story will not be received the way you hoped. Sometimes it will be met with silence. Or resistance. Or misinterpretation.

Tell it anyway—if it brings you closer to yourself.

Do not tether your healing to applause. Do not shrink your truth to protect someone else's version of you.

You share not to be impressive, but to be free. Not to gain followers, but to reclaim your breath.

Alignment is the only outcome that matters.

Your Story Will Evolve—Allow It

You do not owe the world a fixed version of your truth.

You are allowed to change. To heal. To reframe. To reimagine. What you believe about your past will evolve as you grow—and that evolution is not betrayal. It is maturity.

Every time you revisit your story with deeper compassion, you expand your capacity to understand it.

You are not being inconsistent. You are being alive. That is enough.

Let Truth Be Your Legacy

Every time you speak your story aloud, you remind someone else they are not alone.

You become the mirror you once searched for. The voice you once needed. The permission someone else is still waiting on.

Stories have always been sacred medicine. Across oceans and generations, they have been how we survive, remember, and rise.

Your truth is not just for you—it is a gift. It becomes legacy the moment it makes someone else feel less invisible.

A Final Whisper: Your Truth Is the Beginning

You do not have to share everything. You do not have to speak before you're ready. But you do deserve to stop hiding.

Your voice is not too late. Your truth is not too much.

You do not need to be healed to begin telling your story. You only need to be willing to honor it.

Start with what is real. Start with what is ready. Start with the quiet ache that says: I want to be known.

And let that be the beginning.

Of healing. Of connection. Of freedom.

Of you—fully seen.

From One Heart to Another —
Trust the Timing of Your Bloom Letter from a champion

Dear Girl,

If I could sit across from you now, I would take your hand, look you in the eye, and say this gently but firmly:

You are enough.

You are loved.

You are full of possibility.

You carry a light that is entirely your own—and the world needs it, even if it hasn't been fully seen yet.

You don't need to have it all figured out. What you do need is a spark—a curiosity, a passion, a sense that there's something within you worth exploring. Follow that. Even if it seems impractical. Even if others don't understand. That spark is your inner genius.

I spent much of my life following the path laid out for me—excelling in school, earning a Ph.D. in electrical engineering, becoming a senior scientist at the Department of National Defence, and an adjunct professor at Carleton University. On paper, everything looked perfect.

But something was missing. That something was passion.

Through a friend, I discovered real estate investment as a side interest. It began as a hobby—then became a calling. I felt alive and fulfilled helping people make important life decisions and generate wealth through real estate. I realized I was a people person, and my real strength was connecting with people.

At the age of 48, I made a leap that surprised everyone: I left my secure government job and launched my real estate business.

People questioned my choice.

"Wasn't this a waste of your Ph.D.?"

"Are you sure about giving up job security and a pension?"

But I had finally discovered something precious—something that had been quietly waiting inside me all along: passion.

It wasn't an easy decision. I had spent years doing what I thought I was supposed to do: choosing stability and seeking approval. But deep down, I always felt a quiet tug, a longing to do something more aligned with who I really was.

That's why I am writing to you now. I want to tell you—you don't have to wait until midlife to listen to yourself. You don't need to silence your curiosity, or squeeze yourself into a version of success that doesn't feel right. I made the leap late, but you can start tuning in earlier. Your life is yours to design.

And here's what I've come to believe—truths I wish I had known earlier, and that I now want to share with you, so you feel empowered to walk your own path with confidence and grace:

1. Follow your passion—it is your inner genius.

Passion is not a luxury. It's not something reserved for artists or dreamers. It's your compass, your power source, your truth. It reveals what makes you come alive—and when you follow it, you unlock your unique gift to the world. That is your genius.

It may arrive as a whisper or a tug. It may come late in life, as it did for me. But when it does, honor it. Nurture it. It will guide you home to yourself.

2. Grow your confidence—one choice at a time.

I was once an A+ student. I did what I was told. I followed the rules. I cared deeply about what others thought. But confidence doesn't come from approval. It comes from action. From choosing yourself.

I'm still learning to speak to myself kindly: You're doing your best. Keep going.

I invite you to do the same.

3. You don't need to be perfect to be loved.

This may be the most important lesson of all:

You are lovable as you are.

You don't need flawless skin, straight A's, or constant praise.

You don't need to shrink or perform to be accepted.

For years, I chased perfection—trying to be everything to everyone. But I've learned this: we are all flawed and fallible human beings. And we are worthy anyway. So speak to yourself the way you would to a dear friend—with kindness, understanding, and forgiveness. Let yourself be messy, human, evolving. That's where the beauty lives.

4. Seek mentors—and become one.

My journey has been guided by others—people who opened doors, shared wisdom, and believed in me. My father's motto was, "Find joy in helping others." That has become my compass.

Today, I lead a multicultural real estate company with the culture "Care, Give, Serve." We support charities. We host community events. Why? Because success is sweeter when shared. I want to create the kind of support I once needed. So if you're ever unsure, don't stay silent. Ask for guidance. Reach out. And one day, when you can—reach back.

Forging your path won't always be easy. There will be doubt, detours, and days that feel like failure. But if you keep walking—step by step—you'll discover something powerful:

You own your life.

For years, I let others choose for me. I followed the safe road. But today, I make my own decisions. I live by design, not by default. And I wake up every morning excited to help others do the same.

If no one's told you yet—you have the right to dream your own dreams.

You have the power to create something new, something uniquely yours.

And to end, I want to share a poem I wrote:

Let's Dance!
By Helen Tang

When the sun rises,
Let's dance!
Shake every muscle,
Celebrate a new day to come!

When the sun sets,
Let's dance!
Throw all worries,
Free your soul!

When the rain falls,
Let's dance!
Soak up in happiness,
Cheer for rainbow!

When the winter comes,
Let's dance!
Warm up every fiber,
Spring is around the corner!

Whatever season you're in, keep dancing.
Keep listening.
Keep becoming.

Because…
You are enough.
I am enough.
We are enough.

I believe in you.
I'll be cheering for you.
And the best is yet to come.

With all my love,
Helen

PART VII

Rise: Lead with Love

You are here to live, love, and light the way for others.

You are not here just to survive. You are here to lead.

Not the kind of leadership the world often glorifies—where power is loud, and control is mistaken for influence. But a quieter, deeper kind. A leadership rooted in love. Anchored in purpose. Rising from the inside out.

You are not too young. You are not too soft. You are not too late.

The path you have walked—the pain, the beauty, the healing—has prepared you to become the kind of leader this world desperately needs: one who leads not for applause, but from alignment. One who doesn't chase the spotlight but brings light wherever they go.

This chapter is an invitation to claim your place as a leader of love.

A leader who listens deeply.

A leader who lives intentionally.

A leader who sees the humanity in others and honors the divinity in themselves.

Your voice, your vision, your values—they are not random. They are tools for transformation. The things you care about, the dreams that stir your soul, the injustices that break your heart—these are not distractions. They are your map. They are signs pointing you toward your unique calling to serve.

Because leadership is not a title you wait to be given. It is a truth you choose to embody.

You lead every time you stand up for someone who cannot.

You lead every time you show up fully, with compassion in a space that needs healing.

You lead when you say, "I've been there too," and extend a hand back.

This is not about being perfect. It is about being present. Present to yourself. Present to your purpose. Present to your people. And in a world that often chooses fear, your love will be your legacy.

So rise. Not just for yourself. But for the next girl watching you. For the ones still silencing themselves. For the ones who need proof that tenderness and power can co-exist.

Rise.
Lead.
And love—fiercely, gently, brilliantly.

The world has enough noise.
What it needs now… is your light.

From One Heart to Another —
Grace Is a Leadership Strength Letter from a champion

To every girl—the future leaders, innovators, and visionaries who will build a better world,

As I sit down to write this letter to you, I do so with a full and open heart. A heart that has been shaped by joy and struggle, by hope and heartbreak, by powerful mentors and hard-fought victories, by great privilege and quiet moments of self-doubt—and by the lessons learned through every stumble and every step forward.

This letter comes from one woman to another, across time and generations—with the hope it becomes one of many small lights guiding your path, just as others have so generously illuminated mine.

I want you to know something that took me years to fully understand:

You are needed.

Your light, your voice, your values, your dreams—they are not just valid; they are vital. There is no one else in the world exactly like you, and that is your superpower. You were born with a purpose, and I fully believe you have the strength, courage, and brilliance to fulfill it.

Throughout my journey—as a daughter, a sister, a dreamer, a community builder, a co-founder, entrepreneur, director of the board, and now a CEO—I've experienced winding roads, unexpected turns, and what felt like immovable walls. And I've also experienced the kind of fulfillment and impact that comes from finding your voice and using it; from discovering your values and standing by them; from investing in others and receiving the incredible gift of love and support in return.

I want to share four truths that have helped me navigate the complexities of life and leadership. My hope is that they will offer you a steady hand as you blaze your own trail.

1. Dream Big. Boldly. Unapologetically.

Never, ever let anyone tell you your dreams are too big. They belong to you—and they are possible. They matter because you matter. The world is hungry for your ideas, your energy, your spark. And even when the wind pushes against you, even when the road feels lonely or the barriers seem too great, I want you to remember: you can keep going. You can do hard things and succeed.

There were times in my life when I questioned whether I belonged in certain rooms, whether I was the right one to lead, whether I could take the next step. I have stumbled, made mistakes, and learned every day. One of the key learnings: resilience is a muscle, and you build it by using it. Every day, you wake up and take one more step. And then another. Over time, that persistence turns into progress—and that progress becomes impact.

So, please. Dream without limits. And then take action—small steps, big steps, sideways steps if needed—but never stop moving forward.

2. Anchor Yourself in Your Values. Let Them Be Your North Star.

Your values—your truth—are what will carry you through the toughest moments of your life and keep you grounded in the greatest ones. They are what give your life and your leadership meaning.

Early in my career, I found myself in situations where it would have been easier to stay silent, conform, or walk away. But I've learned— through trials and triumphs—that standing by your principles, especially when it's hard, is one of the most courageous and powerful acts of leadership.

Your values are unique to you. They're shaped by your lived experiences, your culture, your passions, and your purpose. They are like your fingerprints—completely yours. Honour them. Speak them. Live them. They will never lead you astray.

3. Get Back Up—Every Time.

You will fall. You will have your heart broken—in life, in work, in dreams deferred, and in moments that don't go as planned. But know this: there is no failure—only learning. Every fall will be a lesson, even when it's really hard and you'd never choose to go through it.

And that's when I learned one of life's most powerful truths: you don't have to rise alone. I didn't. I've been lifted by the critical support of those around me. Sometimes slowly—but I rose stronger. Wiser. More focused, committed, and driven.

Inner strength isn't about being unbreakable. It's about rebuilding. Discovering and deploying grit you didn't know you had. It's about knowing that you are worthy—not because of what you achieve, but because of who you are. And every single time you rise, you inspire someone else to do the same.

So be gentle with yourself. But be fierce in your determination. Never stop learning. Your worth is not tied to perfection. Your power and impact lie in your perseverance.

4. Live with Gratitude. Lead with Love.

There is no force more powerful in this world than love—especially when it's shared freely and courageously. Love for others. Love for your community. Love for yourself.

When we lead with love, we create spaces where others feel seen, heard, and valued. When we lead with gratitude, we recognize the people who help us along the way—and we understand that success is never achieved alone. Everyone has something special to contribute to the world and those around us.

I've been lifted by incredible champions, mentors, friends, colleagues, and partners—people who believed in me even when I couldn't believe in myself. I've seen firsthand the life-changing power of a kind word, a quiet gesture, a moment of grace.

Never underestimate the impact of your kindness. Reach beyond your usual circles to those who feel unseen or unheard. Foster authentic belonging. You can change lives—and in doing so, you will enrich your own more than any accolade, award, or title ever could.

As Maya Angelou so beautifully said—words that have stayed with me more than any other:

"People may forget what you said, they may forget what you did, but they will never forget how you made them feel."

That feeling—that legacy of love—is what I hope to leave behind. It's also what so many have given to me, and for that, I am endlessly grateful.

So, to every girl reading this:

Know that you are already enough.

You already hold power.

You are already equipped with everything you need to create a life of impact, meaning, and joy.

Keep learning. Keep stretching. Keep building.

And please, don't stop dreaming. Because your dreams don't just matter—they have the power to transform this world.

And we need that power.

We need you.

With unwavering belief in you, all that you are and everything you will achieve,
Sonya

CHAPTER 19

To the Girl Who Feels Like She's Never Enough —

You were never meant to be small

You've spent so long trying to shrink yourself. To be agreeable. To be pleasing. To be perfect. You've edited your words, dulled your brilliance, apologized for taking up space—as if being you was too much for the world to hold.

But I want to tell you something you may not have heard enough: You were never the problem.

Your depth, your passion, your voice, your fire—none of it was ever too much. You were just surrounded by people who couldn't see what a gift you are.

Maybe they taught you that being loved meant being quiet.

Maybe they made you believe that worth is earned through achievement, obedience, or sacrifice.

Or maybe they simply never knew how to love themselves—and you learned their habits of unworthiness as your own.

But even in those moments... especially in those moments... your soul never stopped knowing the truth: You were never meant to be small.

Not in your dreams. Not in your heart. Not in your calling. You were born to expand. To speak. To lead. To take up space with love and integrity.

The world needs your kind of power—the kind that lifts others, not crushes them. The kind that leads with grace, not ego. The kind that listens deeply, speaks truthfully, and dares to be seen— fully, vulnerably, without apology.

So today, I invite you to stop measuring yourself by the love you didn't receive. Stop trying to be palatable in a world that was never meant to define you. Stop abandoning yourself just to belong.

You are enough. Not because you did anything to earn it— but because you are.

It's time to step into your fullness. Not with perfection. But with presence. With purpose. With the knowing that your light was never meant to be dimmed.

Shine— not for their approval, but for your own becoming. You were never meant to be small.

With all my heart,
Someone who sees your light—exactly as it is.

Life Lesson:
You Were Never Meant to Be Small

The world layered you with reasons to shrink, beginning from your earliest breath:
Whispers in the nursery: *"Not too loud."*
Corrections in the classroom: *"Use your inside voice."*
Hushed adult warnings: *"Don't speak unless spoken to."*

Even your own heart began to echo those words:
"Better stay small."
"Better stay unseen."
"Better stay comfortable."

But what if your soul was never made for comfort?
What if, instead, it carried a wildness meant to be seen—a voice meant to rise—a courage meant to grow?

This chapter is for the girl who has lived most of her life believing less was safer. For the one who dimmed her brilliance in the name of belonging. For the one who learned early that inhales are louder if remembered.

It ends here.

The Legacy of Smallness

Too often, we inherit not just homes—but patterns.
"Speak only when spoken to."
"Stay out of the way."
"Don't ask for more."

It might not have been malice. It might have been fear. Fear that your brightness would eclipse.
Fear that your voice would overpower.
Fear that your fire would make others uncomfortable.

So the message became: *Better small.*

My own smallness had roots—a war-torn childhood where speaking out meant danger, a refugee journey where invisibility felt like safety. I learned to carry my value quietly, even though inside, a fire burned for justice, for belonging, for change.

At twelve, I won an award but stayed silent on stage. In a room full of people cheering, I refused to claim it. I thought humility meant shrinking.

But humility is not absence. Humility is heart.
Leadership does not require all eyes—it requires one steady eye: your own.

Shrinking Does Not Protect You

Smallness was meant to shield—but it never protected me from feeling unseen or unworthy. If anything, hiding made me more vulnerable to doubt, comparison, anxiety.

The cost of shrinking is high:
You trade your sacred birthright for others' comfort.
You teach yourself that your peace depends on staying invisible.
You carry the exhaustion of performing a version of yourself others can digest.

But there is another way.

Courage to Expand

Your soul wants more: more belonging, more expansion, more freedom to be yourself. Even on your smallest days— when the voice trembles, when the fear speaks louder—your core remains unchanged:

You were never meant to be small. Let us look together at how we begin to reclaim that truth—through presence, love, and radical self-holding.

The Turnaround Story

I was nineteen, in a job interview where I was told I was "too passionate," "too emotional," "too ambitious." I smiled and said, *"Thank you."* But inside, I cried.

I had been taught to hide those parts—the passion, the compassion, the ambition—because they were reminders I was *too much.*

And yet, those were exactly the parts the world needed.

Years later, leading a group of refugee children in a camp, the ones who once told me I was too much were nowhere to be found. What mattered then were the parts I had tried to quiet—my heart, my voice, my courage, my vision.

The world's labels do not define your impact.

Embracing Fullness as Leadership

Leading with love means letting your fullness be your guide.

When you stand fully—no longer apologizing for your height, your tone, your truth—you become a lighthouse. Others will follow. But the glow must begin from within.

Practice presence: let your posture speak confidence, even when your spirit wobbles. Practice speaking your truth: say your name, say what you feel, speak what you see—even in small spaces. Practice visible boundaries: assert your worth. It is not harsh. It is holy.

When Fear Speaks—Let Love Answer

Every time fear speaks, let love be the one who answers:

Fear says, *"They will think you're arrogant."*
Love replies, *"I am here with purpose."*

Fear says, *"Better stay small."*
Love replies, *"My presence has value."*

Fear says, *"You don't belong here."*
Love replies, *"I belong where I am called."*

Fear roars.
Love whispers truth.

Small Actions, Giant Impacts

You don't need to be loud to lead.

Saying no to one thing that drains you is a radical act of self-respect.
Sharing one small idea becomes a tool someone else can use.
Walking into a room as yourself—full force—becomes hope for someone else still holding back.

Your very being breaks generational patterns of hiding.

Reclaiming Your Body, Your Voice

Your worth doesn't live in achievement.
It lives in presence—in the way your hips sit, your gaze holds, your breath carries weight.

Your breath was never meant to shrink. Your ribcage was not designed to fold in. Your voice was never supposed to be hushed.

Start small: Stand tall.
Take your space. Speak your name. Speak your truth.
Let your body remember it was made for impact.

The Grace in Saying, "I Am Enough"

There is nothing more fierce than someone who knows she does not owe the world anything—to prove, to perform, to earn.

There is nothing more free than someone who has ceased defending her worth.

You don't need to be loud. You need to be true.
You don't need permission. You need remembrance.

A Final Invitation

The road of rising is not flawless. You will have moments of shrinking. That's okay.

When that happens: Feel your breath. Press your feet into the ground. Internalize the whisper: *I was not made to be small.*
And rise again.

Closing Reflection

You were never meant to be small.

Your scars, your questions, your dreams—they are not mistakes. They are map lines pointing toward your purpose.

The world needs your voice, your vision, your values.
Your life is your legacy.

So live from where love meets courage.
Speak from the place inside that knows it is enough.
Lead with empathy, with integrity, with openness.

You are not here just to survive. You were made to rise—
to reignite,
to renew,
to revolutionize.
Because you were never meant to be small.

Tools for the Journey:
Awaken to Your Fullness

You were never meant to shrink.

You were meant to rise.

And rising requires tools—not to overpower, but to empower your most authentic self. Tools that invite your heart to lead with compassion. Tools that guide you through uncertainty with courage. Tools that allow you to carry a clear vision of wholeness, rooted in who you truly are.

These are tools to help you live, love, and light the way for others—boldly, gently, unapologetically.

Cultivate Your Inner Witness

When you feel small, you need someone to hold you with tenderness in your own gaze. That someone is your inner witness—the part of you that remembers how bright you are, even when fear dims your spark. Come back to presence by saying, "I see you." Let the words land in your body. Let your breath become your anchor. Return to this quiet practice whenever you feel yourself disappearing.

Declare Your Truth Daily

Leadership is a daily return to truth. Begin each morning with affirmation, not performance. Speak aloud: *I am here. I matter. I carry something sacred.* These declarations do not need to be loud to be powerful. They simply need to be consistent. Over time, they become your soil—steadying your roots in who you are.

Redefine Your Mirrors

Too many of us have lived our lives through mirrors that distort us—mirrors shaped by judgment, comparison, or colonial ideals.

Now, redefine your reflection. Surround yourself with affirming souls, soul-rooted texts, art that reflects your worth, and stories that speak your language. Your mirror should show you more of your truth—not less.

Ground Yourself in Connection

Loneliness can quietly sever us from our purpose. Root yourself daily in what nourishes your heart. Each morning or evening, name three things that brought you joy, beauty, or connection. These may be simple—a shared smile, a moment of silence, the warmth of tea. Let them remind you that you are not alone. You are part of something bigger.

Set Heart-Centered Boundaries

To love others well, you must first love yourself enough to say no. Ask yourself gently: *Does this honour my energy or deplete it?* Boundaries are not rejection—they are clarity. Let them protect the flame within you, so your light continues to burn without burning you out.

Speak Your Full Name

Your name carries your lineage, your dignity, and your belonging. Speak it often. Speak it proudly. Write it down like scripture. Let it remind you of who you are—and who you come from. Your name is not too much. It is your belonging, spoken into sound.

Expand Through Small Acts of Boldness

Boldness does not always arrive in grand gestures. It lives in the quiet choices. This week, choose one small act that stretches you. Say what you've been holding. Reach out to someone you admire. Tell the truth where you once stayed silent. The tremble in your voice is your courage rising.

Embrace Your Softness

You do not need to harden to be strong. Let your softness speak. Let it lead. Offer yourself grace. Allow your tears. Love loudly. Gentleness is not weakness—it is rooted resilience. Let tenderness become your most courageous act.

Lead With Listening

To lead is not to fill a room with your voice—it is to fill a heart with your presence. When someone speaks, pause. Lay down distractions. Listen for what is not said. Let your stillness become a sacred space for others to be seen. That is leadership at its most profound.

Create Your Compass Statements

When the world grows loud, return to soul-rooted truths. Write down a few compass statements that orient you:

- *I lead with love, not fear.*

- *I protect my joy like sacred ground.*

- *I do not abandon myself to belong.*
  Let these guide your decisions when clarity feels far away.

Remember the Ripple Effect

Your light is not just for you. It's for the girl watching you from the shadows. For the woman who still doubts her voice. For the elder who forgot her power. Say to yourself often: *May my becoming awaken hers.* You are not just rising for yourself. You are rising for all of us.

Rest Is a Radical Part of Rising

Rest is a holy interruption to a world obsessed with speed. It is a quiet refusal to perform your worth. Rest to remember your humanity. Rest to feel again. Rest because your joy matters—not just your output.

Bringing It All Together

You are not here to hustle for significance. You are here to live, love, and lead with presence. These tools are not to make you more—they are to return you to your enoughness. Use them whenever the world forgets your value. Use them whenever you forget it yourself.

You were never meant to be small.

You were meant to rise.

And rise you shall—with tenderness, truth, and a light that was never meant to dim.

CHAPTER 20

To the Girl Who's Trying to Please Everyone —

You don't owe the world your silence

I know why you try so hard.
You want to be the glue, the peacekeeper, the one everyone can count on. You want to make things easier, lighter, softer for the people you love. You've become so good at making sure others are comfortable that you've learned to silence the parts of yourself that might make waves.

But here is the truth no one told you: Peace is not the same as people-pleasing. And love is not meant to cost you your voice.

You do not have to agree just to be accepted.
You do not have to smile when you want to speak.
You do not have to carry the weight of everyone else's expectations to be worthy of love.

You are not difficult for having a boundary.
You are not unkind for being honest.
You are not selfish for needing space.

Somewhere along the way, you were taught that love means sacrifice—and it does, in its healthiest form. But sacrifice is not the same as self-abandonment.
You were not born to twist yourself into shapes that make everyone else comfortable while your own soul is starving.

You were born to be whole.

You were born to take up space—with your ideas, your emotions, your longings, your dreams.
The world does not need your silence.
It needs your truth.
Your full, radiant, imperfect, human truth.

And the people who are meant to love you will never ask you to shrink.
They will not need you to disappear to make them feel big.
They will honor your voice as much as your presence.
They will not confuse your boundaries with rejection, or your honesty with harm.

So speak.
Not to please.
But to live.
Not to convince.
But to exist in your fullness.

Let your words return to you. Let your truth stretch its legs. Let the girl who's been keeping quiet finally breathe without guilt.

Because your voice is sacred.
Your needs are valid.
And your worth has never been tied to how well you keep the peace.

You do not owe the world your silence.
You owe yourself your becoming.

With deep love,
Someone who sees your light

Life Lesson:
You Don't Owe the World Your Silence

I used to think that being liked was the same as being loved. That being agreeable made me kind. That being quiet made me good.

It took me years—decades, really—to understand that people-pleasing is not kindness. It is self-abandonment, wearing a smile. And often, the story begins in childhood. Maybe you were the peacemaker, the helper, the "easy" one. Maybe someone in your life needed you to be small so they could feel big. Maybe love was conditional—offered when you behaved, withheld when you had needs. So you learned to perform. You learned how to please.

You learned how to disappear in plain sight.

The Performance of Approval

I know what it feels like to scan a room not to connect, but to calculate—how do I need to show up to be liked here? Should I shrink? Stay quiet? Agree when I don't?

For years, I mistook approval for love. Applause for belonging. But when your worth depends on other people's comfort, you will always fear being too much—or not enough.

So you become a shapeshifter. You water down your voice. You smooth your edges. You overcompensate. You try to be everything for everyone. But the cost?
You start losing yourself.

The Pain of Betraying Yourself

People-pleasing doesn't always announce itself in big moments. Often, it is a slow erosion—so subtle you hardly notice it happening.

You say yes when you want to say no. You laugh at jokes that hurt you. You take the blame to avoid conflict. You swallow your truth to keep the peace.

It feels easier in the moment. But later, in the quiet, when you are alone with yourself, the ache returns. It always does.

And that ache? It is not just because others didn't see you. It is because you stopped seeing yourself. You betrayed your own voice to become someone's version of "nice." You disappeared for their comfort. And the longer you do it, the further you drift from your own truth—until one day, you no longer recognize the reflection staring back.

The Reclamation Begins with One No

The first *no* is the hardest. The first time you say, "I actually disagree." The first time you step back instead of rushing in. The first time you sit with the discomfort of being misunderstood— without overexplaining yourself.

It can feel terrifying. Because for many of us, people-pleasing was a survival strategy. It kept peace in chaotic homes. It helped us navigate school, workplaces, relationships.

But survival is not the same as living.

And the moment you choose your truth over someone else's comfort, you begin to live.

I Remember the First Time I Chose Me

I remember standing on a stage, heart pounding, palms sweating, delivering a speech that felt too bold, too real, too "much." A part of me feared judgment. But another part—the part that had been silenced too long—rose to the surface.

That day, I didn't speak to be liked. I didn't speak to be approved of. I spoke because the truth needed a voice—and mine would do.

I cried afterward. Not because it was perfect, but because it was mine.

That moment changed everything. I realized I could be respected and real. I could be honest and still held. I stopped performing and started living.

Your Truth Is Not a Threat

If you were conditioned to believe that being lovable meant being agreeable, let me say this: You do not have to make yourself smaller to be safe. Your truth is not too much. Your needs are not a burden. Your voice is not a threat.

You are allowed to take up space—in conversations, in decisions, in your dreams.

And if someone walks away because you dared to speak your truth? That is not loss. That is clarity.

The right people will never require your silence as proof of your worth.

Leading With Love, Not Performance

There's a myth that strong women must be unshakable—always composed, always agreeable. But real leadership, heart-led leadership, is not about performance. It is about presence.

It is about standing in your values, even when your voice trembles.

Yes, you may be misunderstood. There will be those who preferred the quieter version of you. But their discomfort is not your responsibility.

Your responsibility is to your peace.
To your integrity. To your voice.

You Are Not Alone in This Unlearning

Maybe right now, you are trying to find your way back to yourself. Maybe your spirit is whispering, *enough.*

If that is you, know this: you are doing sacred work. It takes courage to unlearn decades of conditioning. You will lose some people along the way—but you will find yourself. And that is the most beautiful reunion of all.

You Don't Owe the World Your Silence

You do not have to be everyone's favorite to be free.
You do not have to be palatable to be powerful.
You do not have to disappear to be loved.

You were never created to be convenient.
You were created to be you.

With truth in your bones.
With fire in your spirit.
With a voice that rises—not to overpower, but to awaken.

Speak. Even if your voice trembles.
Say no. Even if your heart races.
Choose yourself. Again and again.

This is not selfish.
This is holy.
This is leadership.

Tools for the Journey:
Choose Truth Over Approval

There is a cost to constantly shrinking yourself for others' comfort. A cost to bending your voice, your vision, your truth around everyone else's expectations. That cost is your freedom. And in the long run, it is your leadership.

To lead with love—the kind that includes you—you must release the belief that you are responsible for everyone's peace at the expense of your own. These tools are here to help you return to your truth, reclaim your presence, and lead with courage, clarity, and compassion.

Recognize the Pattern: The People-Pleasing Trap

People-pleasing is often born from survival. You may have learned to read the room before you learned to read your own needs. It might have kept you safe, helped you feel loved, or earned you praise. But what once protected you may now be keeping you small. Begin to notice the signs: saying yes when your body says no, silencing your ideas in rooms where they belong, avoiding conflict to keep temporary peace, or ignoring your needs to stay liked. Naming these patterns is not about blame. It is about liberation. You are allowed to choose freedom over approval.

Create a Practice of Self-Validation

When you do not feel seen from within, you begin chasing validation outside of yourself. But you are your most consistent witness. Begin each morning with an affirmation that roots you in worth: *I trust my instincts. My truth matters.* In the evening, ask yourself gently: *Where did I abandon myself? Where did I honor myself?* These small, sacred check-ins will build self-trust, one brave moment at a time.

Learn the Language of Boundaries

Boundaries are not punishments—they are declarations of dignity. They do not push people away; they allow authentic connection to flourish. Learn to say: *"I'd love to, but I do not have the capacity right now."* Or, *"I need time before committing."* Or even, *"That's not in alignment for me."* You are not responsible for how others receive your truth—only for speaking it with kindness and clarity. Let your boundaries become an act of love for both yourself and those you lead.

Speak Up—Even When It's Uncomfortable

Speaking your truth might feel unfamiliar, even terrifying. That is not a sign you are wrong—it is a sign you are healing. Your voice may tremble. Your heart may race. Speak anyway. Begin with small acts of honesty: share a feeling you usually hide, voice an idea you are proud of, say "no" with compassion instead of guilt. With each moment of expression, your nervous system learns that it is safe to show up as you.

Anchor Yourself in Purpose, Not Perception

The more visible you become, the louder the opinions may grow. But opinions are not truth. Anchor in your own values. Ask: *What do I stand for? What kind of leader am I becoming? What ripple do I want to leave in the world?* When you lead from purpose, you no longer need to be perfect. You need only to be present. The clarity that comes from within will always outlast the noise that comes from around you.

Practice Sacred Rest from Performance

You were not born to be a performance piece. Rest is not something you earn after proving yourself—it is your birthright. Carve out space where you do not need to be useful to be valuable. Disconnect from expectations, even your own. Sit in stillness. Let your breath come unmeasured. Journal without editing. Let rest become your rebellion. Because a rested woman is a radical force.

Surround Yourself with Truth-Tellers, Not Just Cheerleaders

You deserve to be held in spaces where you are not applauded for pretending, but loved for being real. Seek out those who reflect your truth back to you, even when it is hard to face. People who love your fullness, not your performance. People who remind you that harmony is not worth your silence. These truth-tellers are your sacred circle. Nurture them. Be one of them.

Final Reflection: You Were Not Made to Disappear

You were never meant to dissolve yourself into other people's expectations. You are not here to be agreeable—you are here to be aligned. And when you stop performing, when you speak instead of swallow, when you choose wholeness over acceptance—you free not only yourself, but everyone watching you.

So speak up.
Show up.
Stand steady in the storm.

Because your voice—just as it is—was never too much.
It was always light.

Let it shine.

CHAPTER 21

To the Girl Who Wonders If She Matters —

You Are the Miracle

I know there are days when the weight of the world feels unbearable. Days when you question your place in it. When you wonder if your presence makes any difference at all. If your voice matters. If anyone sees how hard you are trying—just to hold it together, just to make it through.

But I need you to hear this, with no uncertainty:
You are not invisible.
You are not forgotten.
And you are most certainly not ordinary.

You are the miracle.

Not because of what you do.
Not because of how many people you help, how perfectly you show up, or how much you accomplish.
But because you exist. Because you breathe. Because within you lives a heart that still hopes, still cares, still dreams—even after all that tried to quiet it.

Your presence changes the world, whether or not the world says so.

Your kindness softens someone's edges.
Your laughter lifts a moment that was heavy.
Your empathy makes someone feel less alone.

And your story—even if it still feels unfinished—is already a source of healing.

You do not have to be loud to be powerful.
You do not have to be certain to be brave.
You do not have to be anywhere other than where you are to matter.

Because every time you walk into a room—even if no one says it aloud—something sacred arrives with you.
You.

The girl who keeps showing up with her heart open.
The girl who leads with love, even when unsure.
The girl who is rising, learning, healing—softly, bravely, in her own time and in her own way.

That kind of presence cannot be measured by applause. It is deeper. It is quieter. It is eternal.

So when the world feels loud and you feel small—when your reflection looks tired and your spirit questions its worth—

come back to this truth:

You matter because you are here.
You matter because you are becoming.
You matter because you were never meant to be anyone else but the miracle that you already are.

You do not need to earn it.
You already are it.

With love that sees you,
With hope that holds you,
With faith that believes in you—
Always,

Someone who knows:
You are the miracle.

Life Lesson:
You Are the Miracle

You are here to live, love, and light the way for others.

There was a moment—a quiet, almost unnoticeable one—that changed me. I was sitting in a dim room, staring at the cracked edges of a mirror. I wasn't searching for beauty, or strength, or even hope. I was just wondering… if I mattered. If my existence made any difference in the grand tide of life. I had done the work, shown up, smiled through the ache, poured love into others—but on that particular day, I felt invisible.

I whispered to myself, "Does it even matter that I'm here?"

I think that's a question many of us have asked—especially when the world grows silent in its recognition of who we are. Especially when we've given so much of our hearts to others and been met with judgment, indifference, or no response at all.

But here is what I know now:
Your existence does matter.
You are the miracle.

Not because of what you do or how much you give. Not because of how many people applaud you. You matter because you are. Because your breath is a thread in the great tapestry of humanity. Because your story, even in its quietest chapters, is reshaping the world.

There were seasons in my life when I mistook visibility for worth—when I believed that if no one was clapping, then my effort was wasted. But some of the most powerful things we do in this life are the ones no one sees. The whispered prayers. The decision to stay kind in a world that tests our tenderness. The courage to begin again when the last beginning broke us.

I've seen miracles unfold in the most unexpected places. A girl in a refugee camp who still dreamed of becoming a teacher. A woman who lost her child and still found a way to love again. A young person who stood before a classroom, voice trembling, and still dared to speak their truth.

We often wait for the world to name us as valuable. But what if you didn't need permission? What if your birthright was your worth? What if the very fact that you are alive today—with breath, memory, wounds, and hope—means you are already part of something sacred?

The Invisible Miracle

Miracles don't always come wrapped in light. Sometimes, they look like survival. Sometimes, they look like getting out of bed when your soul feels heavy. Sometimes, they sound like a whisper that says: "Try again."

The miracle is that you are still here. Still hoping. Still loving. Still trying. Even after everything.

You've survived more than most people will ever know. You've navigated storms that would have sunk someone else. And yet, you don't see yourself as heroic. You just see yourself as... getting by.

But look closer.

You've chosen love again and again, even when it was hard to receive. You've listened deeply to others while silencing your own cries. You've carried responsibilities that were never meant to be yours, and still found space in your heart to lift others up.

That kind of quiet strength is not ordinary. It is extraordinary. That kind of resilience is not accidental—it is sacred. And that kind of presence? That is a miracle.

Why the World Needs You

There's a reason you feel pulled to help, to heal, to give, to lead.

Your compassion, your intuition, your wisdom born from lived experience—these are not accidents. They are gifts.

Even when it feels like no one is listening, please know this:
The world needs your softness in the face of cruelty.
The world needs your clarity in the middle of confusion.
The world needs your vision—even if others don't understand it yet.

You matter not just because of what you've been through, but because of who you've become through it all. Your voice—tender or bold—shifts something in the atmosphere. Every time you refuse to give up on yourself, someone else watching you learns how not to give up on themselves.

And most of all, you matter because your being—your simple, miraculous being—is enough.

A Love That Cannot Be Earned

Many of us were taught that we must earn our worth. That we must perform for love. That "enough" means never falling apart, never asking for help, always being polished.

But love—real love—cannot be earned. It cannot be performed into being. It can only be received. And receiving begins with believing you are worthy of it, just as you are.

Messy. Healing. Honest.
Whole in ways the world may never fully recognize.

You are not too much.
You are not behind.
You are not late to your purpose.

You are a living, breathing miracle. A rare and radiant presence in a world that often forgets how precious life is. You were never meant to question your belonging here. You were meant to remember it.

Your Light Is the Legacy

At the end of this journey, there is one truth I hope you carry with you—one I wish someone had whispered to me when I first wondered if I mattered:

You do.

Immeasurably.

And the moment you believe it—not just in your mind, but in your bones—is the moment the world begins to shift.

You speak differently. You love more openly. You walk into rooms not to prove yourself—but to be fully yourself.

That is the miracle.
That is the light.
That is your legacy.

So if you've ever asked, "Do I matter? Is the world better because I am here?"—
Let this chapter answer you, deeply and forever:

Yes.
Yes, it is.
Yes, you are.
And yes—we need you.
More than you will ever know.

With all my heart,
For every girl—past, present, and becoming:
You are the miracle.

Tools for the Journey:
Return to Your Worth

There is no greater awakening than realizing you already are what you've been searching for. You do not need to earn the right to exist. You do not need to perform your way into significance. Worth is not something you achieve—it is something you remember. Your presence is not an accident. It is a sacred arrival. And the invitation now is to live like that is true.

This final chapter is not about perfection. It is about integration. It is about letting your worth move from concept to embodiment— from distant idea to daily breath. These tools are not just reflections. They are rituals for your return.

Return to Your Inner Knowing, Again and Again

The world is loud. There will always be more noise than truth—more distraction than clarity. You may forget who you are in the face of other people's expectations, but the truth of your worth is never gone. It waits in silence. It waits in stillness. It waits for you to return.

When the noise becomes too much, pause. Sit for just a few moments with your hand over your heart. Breathe slowly. Ask yourself gently: *What is true right now?* Whisper what your soul most needs to hear: *I am already enough. I am already whole.* The more often you return to this place, the less you will look outside for the answer. You already are what you've been waiting for.

Make Your Life a Love Letter to Your Existence

Instead of asking, *Do I matter?*, begin living like you do. Let every small act become a quiet devotion to your worth. Feed yourself with care, not criticism. Use your voice—not to be right, but to be real. Set boundaries that protect your energy without apology. Rest without guilt. Grieve without shame. Laugh when there is no reason but joy.

Your daily choices are not just tasks—they are declarations. Every time you honour yourself, you are saying: *This life matters. I matter.* Let your living become a love letter to the miracle that is your existence.

See the Sacred in Your Survival

You have survived what others will never see. Loneliness that hollowed your chest. Silence that screamed louder than words. The ache of invisibility. The heartbreak of being misunderstood. And still—you are here.

Take time to name what you've lived through. Write down what you carried in silence. Then write: *And I survived.* Not because your pain defines you, but because your survival deserves reverence. Every scar has something to say. Every wound holds wisdom. When you honour your survival, you transform endurance into embodied strength. This is not about pretending it didn't hurt. It's about letting your story become sacred.

Anchor Yourself in Service, Not Proving

When the question of your worth lingers, the instinct may be to over-give, over-perform, over-please. But significance does not live in exhaustion. You are not here to hustle for love or wear yourself out to feel needed.

Shift from proving to serving. Ask: *How can I show up today with love that includes me? How can I offer what is true, not what is expected?* You do not have to be everything for everyone. You only have to be honest, present, and whole. Let your energy be an offering—not from depletion, but from alignment. When you serve from truth, your presence becomes its own quiet revolution.

Create Rituals That Affirm Your Inherent Worth

Worthiness is not always something you feel. Sometimes it must be practiced before it is believed. It is a remembering—a soft return to what has always been true, even when forgotten. Rituals help the body remember what the mind has been taught to doubt. They bring wholeness into the ordinary, grounding you in the quiet truth that you already belong.

These practices do not require wealth or tools. They do not need a mirror, a journal, or a phone. They only ask for presence. Wherever you are, whoever you are, you can begin here—with what is within reach.

Try these small, sacred invitations:

- When you wake up, place your hand over your heart. Whisper: *I am still here. I matter.*

- If you have a mirror, look into your own eyes and say: *You are the miracle. You are enough.*

- At the end of the day, reflect on one moment you showed up—for yourself or someone else. Even if no one noticed, let yourself feel it.

- If you can write, note three ways you were present, kind, or brave.

- If you have access to a device, set a gentle daily reminder that reads: *You belong here.* When it appears, pause. Breathe. Receive it.

These are not tasks to complete. They are touchstones of return. Repetition softens the old stories. It teaches your nervous system a new truth: *I don't have to earn my place. I already belong.*

And that, too, is a form of healing. Quiet. Unshakeable. Yours.

Speak Kindly to Your Younger Self

There is a version of you that still wonders if she mattered. The girl who once felt invisible. The child who didn't know how to ask for what she needed. She may be quiet now, but she still lives within you, waiting to be seen.

Begin a relationship with her. Write her letters. Place her photo where you can see it. Even if you cannot write or hang a photo, your younger self can still be spoken to, honored, and held. Sit quietly, even for a minute, and picture her—your childhood self in the place you once called home. Speak to her in your heart, or whisper into your hands.

Tell her: *You mattered then. You matter now. You never had to prove your worth. You were always worthy of love.*

The healing begins when you stop ignoring her voice. When you make space for her tenderness. When you remind her that someone finally stayed.

Let Your Light Be Witnessed

There is nothing wrong with wanting to be seen. Visibility is not vanity—it is vulnerability. To say, *Here I am*, is one of the bravest things you can do.

Let yourself be witnessed. Share your story with someone who can hold it gently. Speak your truth in a space that honours it. Let your voice be heard, not because you need permission, but because your presence shifts the room.

You were never meant to disappear. You were never meant to hide. You are not invisible. Your light is not optional. It is necessary.

A Final Reflection

You are not here to wonder if you matter. You are here to live like you do. And when the doubt returns—because it will—may you remember:

You are not here by accident.
You are not defined by what you do, how much you give, or who remembers your name.

You matter because you exist.
Because you breathe.
Because you love.

This world is different because you're in it.
You are the miracle.
And that will always be true

From One Heart to Another —
Live Loud, Laugh Free

Letter from a champion

Dear Suzy Q,

I can see you, in your 11-year-old awkward body, feet dangling in the lake, immersed in another afternoon of daydreaming—sun on your face, book by your side, staring at the ripples in the water and making up stories in your head. Picturing what your future life will hold, the adventures you will have. Your curly hair will outgrow the relentless "Annie" teasing and you will be able to speak out loud without getting caught up in your Rs with your face immediately going a tomato color from the embarrassment and shame of it all, driving you into silent insecurity. You will be on stage with confidence and poise, and you will be taken seriously, not told that you are ridiculous. You will travel the world, living in different places with friends and lovers and your life will be filled with joy and laughter, not constant judgment and anxiety. You will be loved, and learn how to love, unconditionally— overcoming your deep-rooted fear of abandonment. And there will come a time, not too far in your future, that you will you stop feeling so painfully alone in a house filled with people.

You imagine yourself being independently fabulous in your 50s, like both of your grandmothers who had had wonderful (and difficult) marriages with men many years their senior (both gone before you knew them) and found themselves on an unexpected mid-life. A vision of wonderful scarves, red lipstick, and fabulous black boots for walking in the rain. Ginger cookies, Charlie perfume, and rye on the rocks. You will have a once-in-lifetime self-appointed godmother and incredible female mentors throughout your career—those women who shatter glass ceilings, speak their minds, break rules and have unapologetic fun doing it. And you will form contiguous circles of female friends throughout your life, those who make choices that are right for them in motherhood, marriage, and career—and those who chart a legacy in business so that no woman ever need to doubt if she is good enough, smart enough, strong enough to do the things she absolutely wants to do. This is your purpose.

You will see strange lands and travel more than almost anyone you know —rejoicing in every take off and nesting into flights with a good book and calming playlist—the perfect (and sometimes only) time you can be totally and completely alone with your thoughts. You will remember that as a teenager, your dad (who you will lose far too soon and carry so much guilt for) will refer to you as a pterodactyl because of the legend (and according to study of their physiology) that they shouldn't have been able to fly but did so out of sheer wanderlust. You will find this so befitting that it will become your first tattoo.

Some will attempt to douse your fire, extinguish your spirit. Some won't know what to do with you. As a young woman working in technology sitting at a table full of men, you will be called a piece of fluff, and you will go home and cut off all your hair and start wearing turtlenecks. You will be taken seriously ; sometimes you will be taken so seriously that people find you intimidating. This will make you angry. You will be referred to as crazy and hysterical, but you will persevere. You will cry when you are angry, when you are happy, when you are sad, when you are worried. You will cry a lot. And you will laugh a lot—sometimes until you cry, or so much so that you pee your pants and your stomach hurts the next day. Laughter will mend your broken heart. You will laugh at other people who take themselves too seriously, and you will learn to laugh at yourself although this will take awhile so be patient. You will become the funniest person you know.

You will have many false starts at love. You will get it very, very wrong—many, many times. You will love deeply, you will break hearts, and your heart will be shattered. And then through the gifts of twin babes who grow into the most amazing humans the world has seen, you will begin to understand what love actually is. You will expand your heart for the humans who come into your life in so many different ways, and you will surround yourself with unconditional love.

Music will continue to be your medicine and you will use it in all aspects of your life, to motivate, to heal, to convene, to collaborate, and to connect. You will have dance parties by yourself in your kitchen on Saturday mornings, and then with the people you love in the evenings under a fabulous disco ball.

Your self-righteousness will shift into drive and give you a voice. You will use that voice to lift up others and create communities of women everywhere you go. You will write to those women every Friday in a way that can only be described as chicken soup for the feminist soul. One day you will be on a plane and in a somewhat sleepy state when you land. The man who had been sitting beside you will pull your carry-on down out of the overhead and say, "You see, chivalry isn't dead," to which you will look him squarely in the eye and reply (out of nowhere), "I will take pay equity over chivalry any day." There will be a woman a few rows behind who says, "Hear, hear." She will be an inspired part of your tribe.

You will surprise yourself with fearlessness. You will become successful in the ways the world currently measures it, and that success will allow you to bring your entire self to everything you do. You will say yes to jobs that you have no business doing and eventually you will only agree to do something that gives you a full body yes. You will talk about feelings at the office and lead teams of senior leaders in mindfulness exercises (and they will love it). Your personal financial acumen (after a few rough starts) will allow you to live in a state of generosity and bring the people you love on adventures near and far. You will constantly be creating the conditions for fun, while appreciating most the early morning moments of being completely and utterly alone.

You will make many mistakes and let a number of people down. You will carry the word disappointment alive in you like a cancer, until it eats away at your reproductive organs and you have to have them removed. And in this journey you will find courage to share your voice in a different way, finally taking a step into the writing abyss that you had dreamt of for thirty years. And you will find forgiveness for yourself in this process, and forgiveness for others, but for yourself most of all for all the wrongs you had, or had imagined, inflicted on those around you.

You will forget how to daydream in the years you are striving to live in someone else's shoes, but don't worry, the daydreaming will find you again. You will listen to the universe through the wind in the trees and the waves hitting the beach and you will manifest the life you end up living. Through a lot of introspection, therapy, and friendship you will learn how to be present and to accept what is. You will be wonderfully flawed and, eventually, you will be grateful for that too. You will begin to dream about what's next after this so-called success, and you will imagine a place where you can once again spend afternoons with your legs dangling in the water.

Your friend,
Shannon

✦ Becoming the Woman You Were Always Meant to Be

You have done sacred, quiet work. You've remembered, reclaimed, and begun to rise.

And now—before the final chapter—I want you to feel this moment for what it truly is:

Not an ending.
But a threshold.
A return to your soul.
A rising into your purpose.

There comes a moment in every journey when the quiet healing becomes a blazing call.

When the soul, once hidden beneath wounds and whispers, stands tall—not because it has never fallen, but because it has learned how to rise.

You are standing in that moment now.

You have survived the ache. You have walked through the fire. You have met your shadows with compassion.

And now—now you rise.

Not to prove. Not to perform.
Not to be who the world told you to be.

But to become—fully, freely, fiercely—the woman you were always meant to be.

This is the part of your story where you stop shrinking to fit and begin expanding to lead.

But let us redefine what leadership means here.

Leadership is not about titles, applause, or perfect strategies.
It is about presence. Integrity. Love.
True leadership is what happens when a soul remembers who it is,
and then chooses to live out that truth—in every room, in every
decision, in every breath.

It is found in the way you show up, especially when no one is
watching.
It is in the courage to speak the truth, even when your voice shakes.
It is in the compassion you offer—to strangers, to loved ones,
to yourself.
And above all, it is in how you love.

Because in a world aching with division, uncertainty, and fear, it
will not be the loudest voice that leads us forward.
It will be the most human one.
The one that knows how to listen.
The one that knows how to hold grief and possibility in
the same hand.
The one that chooses love—not as an emotion, but as a radical
act of service.

You are not here just to succeed by the world's standards.
You are here to transform the world—one honest conversation,
one bold dream, one healed heart at a time.

Your life, in its totality—your scars, your gifts, your truths—is
not just your own.
It is a lightpost for someone else.
A path forward for the girl watching, waiting, wondering if she is
allowed to rise too.

Yes, you are allowed.
Yes, you are needed.
Yes, the world is waiting.

So as you arrive at this final part of the journey, remember:

This is not the end.
This is your becoming.
This is your rising.

With love in your bones, purpose in your breath, and legacy in your hands—
Lead.
Not someday.
Now.

Final Chapter

The Homecoming of Your Wholeness

To Every Girl — Past, Present, and Becoming

To you—the one who carried whispered wishes inside your scars, the one who learned the languages of grief, hope, and courage—this is our shared homecoming.

You began this journey in the quiet places of your heart—returning to the little girl within you. The one who danced before the world told her to sit still. Who dreamed before doubt had a name. You sat with her, listened to her ache, and whispered back: *You belong.*

You stood brave and faced the weight of your story—its silence, sorrow, and strength. You stopped running from the parts that once felt unbearable. You stopped apologizing for your pain. You met your past not with shame, but with compassion, and said: *What do you need from me now?*

And in that reckoning, you remembered who you are.

You are not broken.
You are breaking open.
You are not too much.
You are the exact amount of light needed for what is coming.

You healed not by rushing, but by resting. You learned that self-love is not a luxury—it is your foundation. You reclaimed softness as a form of power. You discovered that joy is not earned—it is your birthright.

You let yourself rise again. Speak again. Dream again. You understood that your story is not your shame—it is your soul's scaffolding. That your sensitivity is strength. That your fire is sacred.

You realized your voice is not noise—it is direction.
Your dream is not fantasy—it is instruction.
Your grief is not weakness—it is evidence that you have loved.

And somewhere between the cracks and the light, you stopped performing perfection and began embodying wholeness—even in your mess, even in your becoming.

You've come home to yourself.

Here is what I hope you hold close— and what we will carry together:

Your past no longer defines your path.
The wounds that once silenced you now shape your wisdom. Every scar maps how you survived, how you loved, and how you found your way home.

Your presence is more powerful than your perfection.
You don't need to be polished to be worthy. You don't need applause to be valuable. You are enough—fierce and gentle, tender and whole—all at once.

Your dream is not just yours—it is the world's invitation.
Every time you rise, you give permission for others to rise too. When you shine, you light the path for someone else who is still finding their way.

Healing is not a finish line—it's a way of being.
Some days you rise. Some days you rest. Some days you breathe through the breaking. But always, always, you return to the truth: *You matter.*

A Blessing for the One Becoming

May you remember your worth in the stillness, not just in the spotlight.
May you trust your soul's voice over the noise of the world.
May your rest be deep, your hope be loud, and your becoming be rooted in joy.
May your footsteps soften the way for the next girl who wonders if she matters.
And may your life become a light that does not ask permission to shine.

You are not just the girl you were.
You are not even only the woman you are.
You are the bridge between them—
Living. Healing. Rising.

To the girl of the past: *You did your best. I see your courage. I honor your tears. I thank you for surviving.*

To the woman you are now: *You are not behind. You are not late. You are right on time. You are the miracle in motion.*
To the one you are becoming: *The world has not seen your fullness yet. But when it does, it will shift. You were born to make waves—not for applause, but for impact.*

Let them say, "She didn't wait to be chosen. She chose herself."
Let them say, "She led with love, and everything changed."
Let them say, "She lived fully, loved deeply, and left light wherever she went."

Because that is who you are.
You are not just the girl in the story—
You are the author of what comes next.

And your next chapter?
It will be nothing short of extraordinary.

With all my heart,
For every girl—past, present, and becoming—
You are the miracle.
And now, it is time to live like it.

End of book.

Letters from Our Champions – From One Heart to Another

Throughout this book, you'll find letters written by mentors, leaders, and women who once stood exactly where you are. Their words were placed intentionally, not just as reflections, but as companions for each part of your journey. Each letter was chosen to meet you in the themes of that chapter—with truth, tenderness, and strength.

These are their voices. These are their letters. May you find yourself in them.

Champion & Mentor Letters Placement Guide

Letter By	Letter Title	Placement in Book	Why It Belongs Here
Jenny Chen	*To the Girl Who Always Felt Too Much and Never Enough*	After Part III – *Embrace*	A gentle handoff between embracing our stories and awakening our voices—this letter affirms sensitivity as strength and prepares the heart to step fully into its light.
Zel Ali	*Dear Girl Holding Back Her Light*	Before Part IV – *Awaken*	This letter honors the moment many girls begin to dim their light and offers a powerful call to reclaim voice, presence, and truth—just before we rise to awaken.

Karla Biones	*Dear Carmen*	After Part IV – *Awaken*	A beautiful intergenerational reflection that anchors the reader after awakening, reminding us that leadership can be quiet, intuitive, and deeply rooted in love.
Carolina London	*Dear Girl Who Wonders About Her Struggles and Life*	Before Part V – *Heal*	This letter speaks to the girl carrying invisible weight and questions. It opens the door to healing with gratitude, authenticity, and permission to be whole.
Lisa Anna Palmer	*Dear Young Lisa*	After Part V – *Heal*	A lived journey of burnout, resilience, and boundary-setting—Lisa's voice reminds us that healing continues as we grow and that self-love must be reclaimed again.
Austen Williams	*Dearest You*	Before Part VI – *Surrender*	An empowering letter that prepares the reader to trust their path, even when it looks uncertain. Austen invites us to let rejection refine us and purpose propel us.
Dr. Helen Tang	*Dear Girl*	After Part VI – *Surrender*	Helen's story of late blooming and realignment is a powerful echo of surrender—showing that it is never too late to follow your spark or choose a new beginning.
Sonya Shorey	*To Every Girl*	Before Part VII – *Rise*	As we prepare to lead with love, Sonya reminds us that true leadership is grounded in gratitude, values, and lifting others as we rise.
Shannon Lundquist	*Dear Suzy Q*	After Part VII – *Rise*	A wise, funny, and heart-expanding finale—Shannon's letter honors legacy, freedom, feminism, and the fearless joy of being fully, unapologetically yourself.

To Our Dearest Champions — Zel, Karla, Jenny, Carolina, Shannon, Lisa, Sonya, Helen and Austen,

Thank you—for not only sharing your wisdom, but for inviting us into the quiet truths of your becoming.

Through your letters, you took us on a journey—across heartbreak and healing, doubt and daring, silence and boldness. You reminded every girl that leadership begins in the heart, that softness is strength, and that we are allowed to rise on our own terms.

You did not just write to us. You walked with us—through the valleys of uncertainty and into the light of purpose.

Thank you for letting us see ourselves in your stories.
Thank you for helping us remember who we are.

With deep gratitude and love,
Solange
For Every Girl

With special thanks to *(alphabetical order by last name)***:**
My Daughters - Aliyah, Leylah & Samilah Keita
Zel Ali
Karla Biones
Jenny Chen
Carolina London
Shannon Lundquist
Lisa Anna Palmer
Sonya Shorey
Dr. Helen Tang
Austen Williams

To each of you who journeyed through these pages thank you.

Thank you for holding space for every girl you have been, every girl you love, and every girl still rising in this world.

Writing For Every Girl was more than a dream. It was a calling. A sacred invitation to remember, to heal, and to believe again in your worth, your voice, and the beauty of your becoming.

If you are a parent, mentor, educator, or community leader... Let these letters open conversations. Use the chapters as guides. Read them with your daughters, your students, your sisters. As you already know: the way you show up with presence, with love, with listening can change a life.

So thank you! You are part of this story too. Because the world every girl deserves cannot be built without you..

If this book has touched your heart, I invite you to keep the circle going
Share what it stirred in you.
Tell your story. Speak your truth. Hold space for someone else's.
This is how the movement grows voice by voice, heart by heart.

So to you, my friend and to all of us
Let us rise together.

There is an African proverb I hold close to my heart:
"If you want to go fast, go alone. If you want to go far, go together."

With all my heart,
Solange Tuyishime Keita

In Full Gratitude
To My Family—My Heart, My Anchor, My Home,

You have been my greatest cheerleaders—long before the world knew my name, long before the stages and the sashes. You have seen every version of me: the little girl with wild dreams, the woman with weary shoulders, and the warrior who dares to rise again and again. Through every leap I've taken—whether graceful or trembling—you have been there, arms open, hearts steady, holding space for me to fall, and rise, and try again.

You have lifted me when I could not lift myself.
You have believed in me when my belief wavered.
You have reminded me of who I am when the noise of the world grew too loud.
In my most celebrated moments, you clapped the loudest. In my most challenging seasons, you stood the strongest.

When the weight of the dream felt heavier than expected, you didn't ask me to stop—you held me closer, whispered strength into my spirit, and said, *"Keep going. We've got you."*

To my children—you are the light behind every 'why' in my life. Your love is my courage. Your laughter, my healing. Watching you grow gives me the strength to continue building a better world - thank you for the dance breaks in between every chapter.

And to my partner—my heart's safe place, my mirror and my strength—I know, without question, that you were sent into this world specifically for me. You are the steady ground beneath my boldest dreams. You see me fully and love me gently, fiercely, and without conditions. Your belief in me is the quiet power behind every brave step I take. Loving you is one of life's greatest gifts.

Thank you—for catching me, for covering me, for celebrating me, for reminding me that I never walk alone.

Everything I do is rooted in the love you have given me.

And for that, I will always carry you with me.

With all my heart,
Solange

LET'S KEEP WALKING TOGETHER

I am so grateful you are here—truly.

For Every Girl was written as a gift of
hope, healing, and becoming.

As a gift from my heart to yours, may these words serve as gentle
companions—to nourish your spirit, inspire your journey,
and remind you that you are never alone.

Whether you are reading for yourself, for a girl you love,
or for the woman you are still becoming—
may these pages continue to walk beside you,
with tenderness, courage, and light.

I look forward to continuing this journey together, as we
build a world where every woman and girl can thrive—
and authentically belong.

✦ MissSolange.com

www.ingramcontent.com/pod-product-compliance
Lightning Source LLC
Chambersburg PA
CBHW061138120626
46546CB00005B/1835